Renewable Energy Top Markets for U.S. Exports 2014-2015

United States Department of Commerce

This page intentionally left blank

Table of Contents

This page intentionally left blank

Executive Summary and Findings

The renewable energy sector promises continued growth for the foreseeable future, reaching $7 trillion of expected cumulative global private-sector investment between 2012 and 2030. Despite some short-term challenges, growth is expected in each renewable energy subsector, including wind, solar, geothermal, biomass, hydropower, and renewable fuels – albeit at different rates. To better position U.S. exporters of these technologies for success in international markets, the U.S. Government launched the ambitious Renewable Energy and Energy Efficiency Export Initiative (RE4I) in December 2010. This *Renewable Energy Top Markets Report* is an important commitment of the RE4I. Intended to provide high-level information regarding key potential export markets for American companies, it provides a tool to steer exporters towards those markets where they may be most effective.

When President Obama announced the National Export Initiative (NEI) in 2010, he did so with the ambitious goal of doubling total U.S. exports over five years. To accomplish this goal, certain high-growth sectors, like renewable energy, needed to increase their exports more substantially. For this reason the U.S. Department of Commerce launched the Renewable Energy and Energy Efficiency Export Initiative (RE4I) with 11 other U.S. Government agencies.

In addition to improved financing, enhanced market access, and more strategic trade promotion, a fundamental pillar of the RE4I was – and remains – a renewed effort to improve two-way communication with the U.S. renewable energy industry. Over the last three years, several new initiatives have helped policy-makers gather direct feedback on the challenges faced by U.S. exporters overseas. New forms of communication now provide industry with updated information on news, upcoming events, and market research more frequently and of higher quality.

This report provides detailed analysis of ten key potential markets, contains six subsector-specific snapshots, and ranks 75 different markets in terms of expected exports through 2015. Information is provided for the overall renewable energy sector and by subsector. The report reflects ITA's commitment to rethink and improve our approach to providing U.S. exporters the specific, timely, and impactful information they need to succeed in foreign markets, ultimately leading to economic growth for communities and supply chains across the United States.

Using the Top Markets Report

The RE4I placed a special emphasis on helping small-and-medium sized enterprises (SMEs) overcome the hurdles to entering new markets. International markets can be daunting, especially for an SME, which is why most small exporters, when they do export, sell their products or services to only one market – typically Canada or Mexico. For such companies, the *Top Markets* report provides a high-level assessment of different market opportunities, allowing exporters to compare markets against each other and develop a more coherent, targeted export strategy.

Please note that rankings in the study [see Figure 1] are based solely on projected exports from the United States through 2015. Company-specific priorities may vary. In other words, just because a market ranks highly

---

Figure 1: Ranking of Markets for Total U.S. Renewable Energy Exports through 2015

1. Canada	11. Netherlands	21. Jamaica
2. China	12. South Africa	22. Venezuela
3. Brazil	13. Kenya	23. Russia
4. Chile	14. Israel	24. Guatemala
5. Mexico	15. India	25. Italy
6. United Kingdom	16. Korea	26. Uruguay
7. Nigeria	17. Japan	27. Costa Rica
8. Peru	18. Denmark	28. Vietnam
9. Belgium	19. France	29. Turkey
10. Philippines	20. Colombia	30. Germany

Figure 2: Renewable Energy & Energy Efficiency Exporter Portal

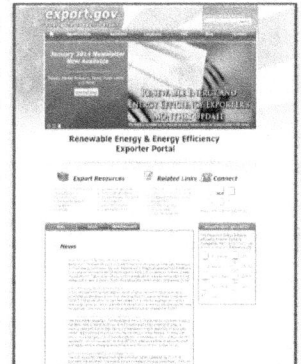

For updated information programs, opportunities, market research, and news from across the U.S. Government, visit our website at: www.export.gov/reee.

The site provides:

 New *Market Intelligence Briefs*

 Information upcoming webinars, trade events, and missions

 A U.S. Government Resource Guide for renewable exporters

The Exporters' Portal is also supplemented by a monthly e-newsletter that highlights new information available on the website. Interested parties can register at www.export.gov/reee and click on the link to the "RE&EE Exporters e-Update."

---

on ITA's list of top export markets, it may not be the right market for your particular technology. For more granular analysis, ITA strongly encourages potential exporters to consult with their local U.S. Export Assistance Center [see http://export.gov/usoffices for contact information].

Moreover, each subsector faces different competitive challenges and each possesses various market characteristics that require export strategies to be highly nuanced and tactical in their implementation. In fact, the renewable energy sector is still so reliant on policy that any change in incentives – whether positive or negative – will have an almost immediate impact on a market's ability to attract clean energy investment which would result in export opportunities.

Exporters should have a firm understanding of a market's policy environment before developing a market entry strategy. Although this report provides a baseline of information, given the dynamic nature of policy environments, exporters are strongly advised to consult with in-country U.S. embassies or consulates in their market of interest for more up-to-date information. ITA also periodically releases detailed *Market Intelligence Briefs*, which provide information on specific policies, changing market dynamics, and key contacts within a country. These documents are available on ITA's Renewable Energy and Energy Efficiency Exporters' Portal [see Figure 2].

The Nature of U.S. Renewable Energy Exports

The *Top Markets* report identifies key trends that will have an impact on both the makeup of U.S. renewable energy exports through 2015 and the elements of an effective strategy for delivering exported products or services to international buyers.

Over the next two years, for example, ITA expects wind energy to overtake solar as the leading renewable energy sector for U.S. exports. This is consistent with an oversupply of wind turbine manufacturing capacity and demonstrates the growing reliance on exports for the sector – a fact supported by strong anecdotal evidence.

Our analysis indicates that the wind subsector will account for nearly 32 percent of all renewable energy exports through 2015, followed by ethanol (27%) solar (19 percent), hydropower (14 percent), biomass pellets (7 percent), and geothermal (2 percent). These figures highlight the broad export profile of the U.S.-based renewable energy industry, as exports are projected in every technology subsector.

It is important to note that ITA's *Top Markets* analysis only considers the export of *products*, which are easier to track using harmonized tariff system codes. The export of *services*, however, may provide an even greater opportunity in many countries. Based on work recently undertaken by the U.S. International Trade Commission, ITA believes service exports are closely correlated with the export of products into markets. The ranking of markets offered in the analysis should thus provide exporters an adequate assessment of overall renewable energy export potential by market.

While the export base of the U.S. renewable energy industry is varied, incorporating several facets of a deep supply chain, the destination of most exports is highly concentrated. When all subsectors are combined, the top 10 markets are expected to account for three-quarters of all U.S. renewable energy exports through

---

Figure 3: Differentiated Strategies for Different Market Dynamics

Characteristic	Potential Export Strategies	Examples
Large U.S. share in large RE market	• Likely to find considerable interest in purchasing products or services • Focus on meeting as many potential buyers or partners as possible	Canada
Small U.S. share in a large RE market	• Must understand if lack of market share is due to competitiveness constraints or protectionist barriers. • Report market access barriers to local U.S. Department of Commerce staff • Find niche opportunities for products in markets without protectionist policies in place	China Japan UK India Brazil Italy
Large U.S. share, but small RE market	• Participate in market development activities • Position company early for when market begins to develop	Mexico South Africa
Small U.S. Share in a small RE market	• Understand that opportunities could be sparse and expect few other American companies to succeed	Paraguay Sri Lanka

2015. The top 30 markets, shown in Figure 1, will account for nearly 96 percent of all exports in the sector. Canada alone will account for 32 percent of all U.S. exports, highlighting the importance of its growing renewable energy market and geographic proximity.

In many markets, only one or two subsectors are expected to account for the majority of U.S. exports. High ethanol demand, for example, drives the rankings of Brazil, Nigeria and Peru. In other markets – namely, China – the pace and scale of investment in renewable energy will support exports, even if individual exporters capture only a small share of the overall market.

Understanding Renewable Energy Markets
ITA encourages markets to be viewed in terms of two variables – import market size and market share [see Figure 3]. A market's "score" on these variables can guide exporters in determining the types of activities that can be effective in certain markets. For the remainder of the study, markets are therefore referenced in terms of their market size and the share of the import market expected to be captured by U.S. exporters.

If a market is large and U.S. firms enjoy considerable market share, then exporters can be assured that business is possible and that meeting potential buyers or partners should be the primary focus of their efforts. The U.S. Government can help facilitate such meetings through trade missions, reverse trade missions, certified trade shows, and other traditional export promotion activities.

In markets that are large, but in which the United States enjoys only a small share of the import market, exporters must consider whether the lack of market share is based on insufficient competitiveness – i.e., the market demands products that most U.S. companies cannot sell competitively; or, whether U.S. products are kept out of the market by protectionist policies. If the latter is true, then exporters may want to consider exporting to another market, while U.S. Government agencies work to open the market to U.S.-made goods and services. If the former is true, then export opportunities may be limited to niche or high-tech products that are not commonly found in the market.

In markets where the United States enjoys considerable market share, but whose overall imports are low, export opportunities may be limited in the near-term. Exporters are nonetheless encouraged to monitor development closely and work towards integrating themselves in the market, such that when development occurs they are well positioned for success. Signs that the renewable energy market is emerging include a government's effort to spur increased deployment and/or consumption through policies and incentives. Several Latin American markets fall into this category and will be targets for trade policy missions, technical capacity building, feasibility studies and other market-growing activities from the U.S. Government.

Finally, some markets are neither large nor support significant U.S. market share. In a time of tight resources, U.S. Government export promotion efforts in these markets will be limited. For companies that may have a personal contact or can offer a specific technology, these markets may still provide some export value, although few American firms are expected to compete productively.

Challenges Facing U.S. Renewable Energy Exports
When designing export strategies, U.S. companies should be mindful of the challenges facing U.S. renewable energy exporters in international markets.

First, although many renewable energy technologies have been invented or developed in the United States, other countries now enjoy considerably more manufacturing capacity in the sector. Companies in these markets often benefit from increased economies of scale and have a manufacturing base to export from when international opportunities arise. This often puts U.S. firms at a disadvantage when competing abroad; a disadvantage that must often be overcome with higher quality products or services.

Second, protectionist policies like local content requirements and high tariffs limit demand for products imported from the United States. India, South Africa, Brazil, and Saudi Arabia have all used some form of policy to limit opportunities for foreign manufacturers to compete in their markets. The United States is committed to enforcing international trade obligations and using existing trade agreements and trade policy forums to address trade barriers when they arise.

When exporters encounter a trade barrier in a foreign market, they are encouraged to report it to the U.S. Embassy or Consulate in the market, or to a local U.S. Export Assistance Center. U.S. Government officials are prepared to advocate for U.S. companies in overseas markets and can sometimes help facilitate arbitration of disputes involving U.S. exporters.

Getting Support from the U.S. Government

The most recent *Annual Review* of the RE4I found that under the initiative the U.S. Government has improved the availability of export financing for the renewable energy sector, facilitated the opening of new markets for U.S. goods and services, more strategically linked buyer and sellers of American technology, and enhanced communication between U.S. Government agencies and the renewable energy industry as a whole. In fact, while all 23 of the RE4I's initial commitments have either been achieved or are in the process of implementation, the lasting legacy of the Initiative is its whole-of-government approach to providing exporters the services they need to be successful overseas.

Exporters are therefore encouraged to use the *Top Markets* report as a tool and a first step in analyzing different opportunities, but to work directly with U.S. Government agencies most relevant to their needs. For example, the Department of Commerce's International Trade Administration has offices in nearly 100 cities and at 72 embassies and consulates around the world – in addition to sector specific analysts in Washington, DC.

Additionally, each U.S. Government agency involved in the RE4I can offer specific programs to support U.S. companies looking to sell products and services abroad. A guide to U.S. Government export promotion programs from across the RE4I agencies can be found at www.export.gov/reee/guide [see Figure 6].

Methodology

Accurately assessing renewable energy trade is difficult. The lack of trade codes often leads to inexact conclusions. Coupling projections of trade with future installation targets – either by technology or country – is often even more problematic given the sector's reliance on government policy. ITA has sought to be clear about the assumptions made in its analysis and welcomes commentary on ways to improve the *Top Markets Study*.

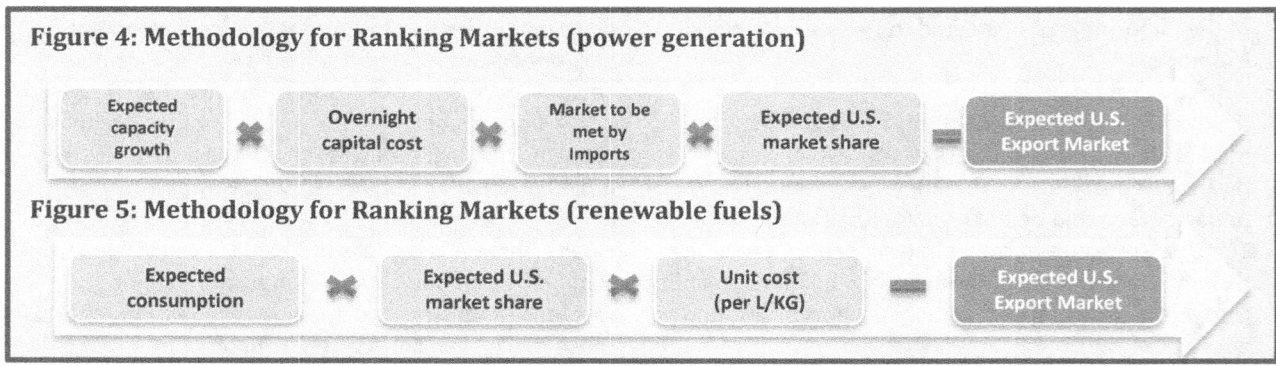

Figure 4: Methodology for Ranking Markets (power generation)

Expected capacity growth ✖ Overnight capital cost ✖ Market to be met by Imports ✖ Expected U.S. market share = Expected U.S. Export Market

Figure 5: Methodology for Ranking Markets (renewable fuels)

Expected consumption ✖ Expected U.S. market share ✖ Unit cost (per L/KG) = Expected U.S. Export Market

To project the size of each country's expected imports from the United States, ITA used the formulas described in Figure 4 and 5. For each market, ITA estimated the projected capacity of installations for power generation technology expected in 2014 and 2015, as well as the consumption of biomass pellets and ethanol. The value of power generation investments was based on estimated costs from the National Renewable Energy Laboratory. ITA then estimated the proportion and value of the market likely to be captured by imports, as well as the percentage of imports expected to be captured by U.S. companies. For renewable fuels, the volume of U.S. exports could be directly compared to the consumption levels. The value was calculated based on the average unit price for U.S. exports of these commodities in each market.

Through these formulas, ITA was able to calculate a projected export market for each country and each subsector, allowing markets to be compared against one another. As more sophisticated data is developed, ITA will continue to update and improve its methodology, providing colleagues and stakeholders a more granular depiction of export opportunities.

A Few Caveats
The technologies used to produce power from biomass were excluded from the study, because the sector's diversity made calculations difficult. The term "biomass industry," for example, can be used to describe a wide range of technology solutions, including traditional biomass, waste-to-energy, and biogas – with each technology using different equipment for the production of electricity. The fact that ITA did not include these biomass-related technologies in this edition of the *Top Markets Study* should not be interpreted as a vote of low confidence in exports from the biomass industry. In fact, some countries that already have abundant natural resources for pellets, such as residues from the timber industry in Southeast Asia, may be suitable markets for biomass power equipment.

Data for certain subsectors was not available for all countries for a variety of reasons. The number of countries pursuing geothermal power, for example, is limited by availability of natural resources. In certain instances, the lack of consumption data limited ITA's ability to consider a market, as was the case for most renewable fuels markets outside of Europe.

Figure 6: A Guide to U.S. Government Export Financing Programs

Financing is often critical for securing or completing an export contract. The Overseas Private Investment Corporation (OPIC), the Export-Import Bank of the United States (Ex-Im Bank), the U.S. Department of Agriculture (USDA) and the Small Business Administration (SBA) offer programs like the ones below that can help U.S. renewable energy exporters compete effectively in foreign markets.

Export financing
- Working capital loan guarantees (SBA, Ex-Im Bank) – enable exporters to finance materials, labor, and overhead to produce goods or services for export.
- Other export loan guarantees (USDA, SBA, Ex-Im Bank) – provide U.S. government-backed guarantees for commercial banks that make international loans.
- Project and structured finance through direct loans (Ex-Im Bank) – involves long term arrangements for funding large U.S. investments that emphasize exports in both developed and emerging markets.
- Export credit insurance (Ex-Im Bank) – enables U.S. exporters to offer short- and medium-term credit directly to their customers during the pre-and post-shipment phases.

Investment financing
- Project finance through direct loans and loan guarantees (Ex-Im Bank, OPIC) – provides medium- and long-term financing for large- and small-scale renewable energy projects involving U.S. investors in emerging markets.
- Political risk insurance (OPIC) – used to mitigate political or sovereign risks for U.S. investors, operators, and lenders (e.g., expropriation, political violence, currency inconvertibility, and breach of contracts with foreign government-owned entities,).

For more information, visit: www.export.gov/reee/guide.

Case Studies
ITA identified the following ten countries from the top 30 for in-depth case studies: Brazil, Canada, Chile, China, India, Italy, Japan, Mexico, South Africa and the United Kingdom. The markets represent a range of countries to illustrate a variety of points – not the top markets overall. The full list of rankings, as well as the full subsector rankings, is located in the Appendix. ITA also developed detailed case studies for the wind, solar, geothermal, hydropower, biomass pellets, and ethanol industries – the six subsectors included in the report's analysis.

This page intentionally left blank

Country Case Studies

The following pages include country case studies that summarize U.S. renewable energy export opportunities in selected markets. The overviews describe U.S. renewable energy export potential in each market, as well as opportunities by subsector. Each case study provides a high-level overview of the challenges exporters may face in the market and highlight upcoming trade events that exporters may consider as part of a market entry or market development strategy.

In addition, contact information for the U.S. Foreign and Commercial Service staff responsible for supporting U.S. renewable energy exporters in the market is provided. Exporters are encouraged to seek more detailed, updated information from ITA when developing specific export plans.

This page intentionally left blank

Brazil

Overall Rank: **3**

Type: Large Market; Large Market Share

Brazil is South America's largest clean energy market. It generates nearly 80 percent of its electricity from renewable sources (including large hydro); and long-term market growth remains all-but-certain. Yet, exports from the United States are unlikely to keep pace with the size of Brazil's overall market due to substantial and intensifying trade barriers. Exporters are likely to find significant demand for their products and services, but often will need to partner with a local entity or utilize Export-Import Bank financing to make deals attractive to Brazilian buyers.

Sub-Sector Rankings

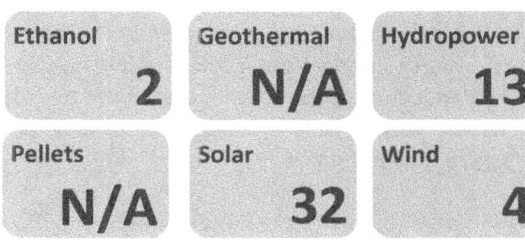

Ethanol	Geothermal	Hydropower
2	**N/A**	**13**

Pellets	Solar	Wind
N/A	**32**	**4**

Brazil's commitment to renewable energy is strong, driven by both its immense renewable energy resource potential and rising energy demand. New clean energy investment in Brazil totaled $5.34 billion in 2012,[1] more than any other Latin American country.

While no specific legislative targets exist, Brazil's "Ten-Year Energy Plan," published in 2011, envisions 18 GW of new renewable energy capacity being brought online by 2020.[2] Given Brazil's existing manufacturing capacity, meeting this target will require the use of both imported and domestically produced technologies. However, many of the Brazilian Government's incentives are geared towards supporting locally-sourced products, making export projections difficult.

Should policies including high import tariffs and local content requirements be removed, Brazil would likely be the most important export market for U.S. renewable energy products and services. Even with such policies, Brazil ranks third on ITA's list of top export markets due in large part to several sectors projected to benefit from opportunities through 2015 and particularly the significant projected ethanol exports.

Overview of the Renewable Energy Market

With growth occurring in almost every energy subsector, large hydropower still accounts for the vast majority of Brazil's energy capacity. Large hydropower dams account for 84 GW of Brazil's total energy

capacity. Other renewable energy technologies account for 15.8 GW of capacity, including 9.84 GW for biomass and waste-to-energy; 3.69 GW for small hydropower; and 2.46 GW of wind power.[3] Additionally, Brazil is a major global producer of ethanol, second only to the United States.[4]

Since its successful 2002 "Program of Incentives for Alternative Energy Sources (PROINFA)," which resulted in 3.1 GW of new renewable energy generation, Brazil has used a broad range of policies to encourage the deployment of renewable energy. These include guaranteed 20-year power purchase agreements, biofuel blending mandates, low-interest financing, and tax-based incentives.[5]

In 2009, PROINFA was replaced by a reverse auction system, through which developers seeking to build renewable energy projects compete against proposed conventional energy projects in regular tenders.[6] The reverse auctions have reduced the price paid by Brazilian consumers for renewable energy, as developers are incentivized to offer the lowest possible cost. The focus on price competition, however, has limited opportunities for solar or other higher priced technologies. Brazil has therefore held biomass- and wind-specific auctions to encourage the deployment of these technologies.[7]

Following a November 2013 auction that was unsuccessful in getting solar developers to offer prices below the Government's price point, a consortium of Brazilian energy companies called for solar-only auctions. Their proposal called for auctions that were similar to those afforded the wind and biomass industries and would be similar to the recent successful solar-only auction held in the State of Pernambuco, which resulted in 123 MW of new solar development.[8] Based on the initial negative reaction of the Brazilian Government's Energy Research Company, however, it is unlikely that such auctions will occur in the near-term at the national level, likely limiting opportunities for utility-scale solar development.[9]

Challenges and Barriers to Renewable Energy Exports

The need for developers to offer electricity at the lowest possible cost makes importing renewable energy technology from the United States commercially difficult. As a result, to date most U.S. exports have been in the form of services and high value-added products that are not available domestically.

The situation is aggravated by significant import barriers. Brazil maintains a 14 percent import tariff on wind turbines, component parts for the wind industry, and hydropower turbines. It also charges a 12 percent tariff on imported solar equipment, both PV and thermal.

The most important challenge, however, pertains to financing. The lending practices of Brazil's development bank, Banco Nacional de Desenvolvimento Econômico e Social (BNDES), pose a significant hurdle to U.S. exports. BNDES plays a major role in financing Brazil's renewable energy growth and is among the largest lenders to the clean energy industry globally, disbursing nearly $29 billion for renewable energy projects between 2007 and 2011.[10]

While there is no explicit local content requirement for participation in Brazil's renewable energy power auctions, BNDES uses local content rules in determining which companies qualify for its low-cost credit. Since BNDES provides the most favorable financing terms, its financing creates a *de facto* local content requirement for the Brazilian market. To illustrate this point, out of the 81 operating wind farms in Brazil, the only one that has thus been developed without BNDES financing was financed by the Chinese Development Bank and used Chinese-manufactured turbines.[11]

In December 2012, BNDES amended its local content requirements for wind projects, making those requirements far more stringent. These requirements include a roadmap for compliance, with each phase requiring a higher percentage of local content. By 2016, BNDES aims to complete an entire Brazilian wind manufacturing value chain in-country – severely limiting the potential for wind product exports from the United States.

Some export deals are nevertheless possible, particularly when facilitated by Ex-Im Bank financing. A recent $32.1 million Ex-Im deal that helped LM Wind export wind blades from its Arkansas-based facility to Brazil is a great example.[12] Exporters will likely have to use similar methods to attract buyers, unless local content restrictions are removed or significantly weakened.

Opportunities for U.S. Companies

Ethanol
While Brazil is a major ethanol producer, it is also a significant market for American ethanol exporters. The reasons are twofold: Brazilian consumption of ethanol is extremely high; and consumers are price conscious because they can choose their blend at the pump. In particular, demand in Northeast Brazil for imported ethanol is strong and should remain a driver of ethanol exports into the future. Exports, however, are closely tied to weather, making future projections difficult. During periods of drought or a smaller-than-usual sugar cane harvest, Brazil imports substantially more ethanol from the United States – as was the case in 2011, when the United States exported $1.2 billion worth of ethanol to Brazil, up from just under $300 million in 2010.

Wind
By the end of 2012, Brazil had over 7 GW of additional wind capacity in a pipeline of projects scheduled to be completed by 2016.[13] While local content requirements and import tariffs limit the opportunity for exporting wind products, service exporters may find some opportunities working with developers of these projects. Wind resource mapping, wind turbine design, and assessing environmental impacts of wind farms should all provide opportunities for U.S. exporters.

Notably, Brazil does not currently manufacture small wind turbines, a market segment that enjoys considerable U.S. competitiveness. As Brazil gears up to host the World Cup in 2014 and the Olympics in 2016, promoting the use of small wind turbines may help create additional opportunities for U.S. exporters.

Solar
Little development has occurred to date in Brazil's solar market, in which total installed capacity was just 7.5 MW at the end of 2012. However, 25 new solar projects totaling 967 MW applied to the Brazilian regulator, Agencia Nacional de Energia Eltrica (ANEEL), for permits in the first half of 2013 alone; and since 2011, *Bloomberg New Energy Finance* reports that over 3.9 GW of solar permits have been requested. As these projects move to completion, some export opportunities should become available, although total solar exports to Brazil will remain limited into the medium-term.

Hydropower
Brazil offers opportunities for U.S. hydropower exporters. However, the legal disputes surrounding the Belo Monte hydropower plant currently under construction are likely to hinder the development of future large hydropower projects.

Two market segments likely hold the most promise for U.S. exports through 2015: small and medium hydropower equipment; and hydropower services. Though Brazilian and Argentine suppliers dominate the large hydropower market, U.S. exporters enjoy considerable market share in the small and medium-sized hydropower market.

Brazil's hydropower reserves hit historically low levels in 2012. Ensuring that the country's existing facilities are producing the most power possible, either through retrofits or system optimization, should provide American service exports with new opportunities.

Upcoming Renewable Energy Trade Events for Exporters interested in Brazil:
- **Brazil WindPower;** *August 26-28, 2014* – Rio de Janeiro
- **Intersolar South America;** *August 26-28, 2014* – Sao Paulo
- **Fenasucro/Agrocana;** *August 26-28, 2014* – Sertãozinho
- **HydroVision Brazil;** *October 21- 2014* – Sao Paulo

U.S. Foreign Commercial Service Contact Information: Igly Serafim
Commercial Specialist
Email: igly.serafim@trade.gov
Tel: 55-11-3250-5187

For more information, please visit: www.export.gov/reee or www.export.gov/brazil.

This page intentionally left blank

Canada

Overall Rank: 1

Type: Large Market; Large Market Share

Canada ranks #1 on ITA's list of top renewable energy export markets through 2015. Over the next two years, Canada will likely account for nearly one-third of all U.S. renewable energy exports. Its proximity to the United States and the close commercial relationship many U.S. suppliers enjoy in Canada provide exporters a favorable environment to sell their products or services. Local content requirements in Ontario and Québec, however, threaten to undermine U.S. export competitiveness and may pose a significant barrier for some renewable energy exporters.

Sub-Sector Rankings

Ethanol	Geothermal	Hydropower
1	N/A	1

Pellets	Solar	Wind
9	1	2

Over the past several years, Canada has undergone dramatic changes in its energy sector, including new renewable energy development that has arisen alongside – and in some cases as a result of – the expansion of unconventional fossil fuels. For the foreseeable future, Canada will continue to be an energy superpower, producing clean energy, but also investing heavily in oil sands and shale gas development.

Estimates indicate that Canada will need 42 GW of new generating capacity to both meet expected demand increases (although minimal compared to other countries) and replace existing generation capacity from plants that will be decommissioned over the next two decades. Given the interwoven nature of U.S. supply chains in Canada, this development foretells significant future exports. Unfortunately, Canada's two most import provinces for renewable energy to date – Ontario and Québec – maintain strong local content requirements, which can limit opportunities for American exporters.

Overview of the Renewable Energy Market

Most of Canada's clean energy policies are created and enforced at the provincial level. In provinces with effective policies, growth in the renewable energy sector has been relatively strong. British Columbia's smart metering program, Ontario's Feed-in-Tariff (FIT)

regime, and Québec provincial clean energy mandate have all led to increased investment in the sector.

To date, Ontario and Québec have been the most supportive provinces for renewable energy. Ontario's Green Energy and Green Economy Act of 2009 established a strong FIT scheme that facilitated the installation of 4.5 GW of new renewable energy capacity in just four years. When it was enacted, the FIT program targeted the installation of 10.7 GW of new non-hydropower renewable energy by 2018 and 9 GW of new hydropower capacity by 2030, putting Ontario on track to be a key global clean energy market.[14]

In 2012-2013, an updated FIT program recorded a slowdown and is currently under review for possible additional changes. It remains to be seen whether Ontario can maintain its attractiveness to renewable energy investors with its new FIT rules in place. Early indications show that other markets have become more attractive, with investment likely waning in Ontario as a result.

In Québec, the provincial Energy Strategy mandates that an additional 4 GW of new wind energy and 4.5 GW of hydropower capacity be brought online by 2015. To support both goals, the Province of Québec launched a cap-and-trade program in January 2013, although the impact of the program remains unclear.

Some analysts believe that over time the program will support additional renewable energy development, but ITA remains skeptical that the cap-and-trade program will have any more than a marginal impact on the sector.

Renewable energy deployment in other provinces remains mixed. Nova Scotia implemented a community FIT accessible to municipalities, First Nation communities, and not-for-profit groups. Saskatchewan has extended its net metering rebate program for projects of less than 100 kW. And New Brunswick has a renewable energy target in place that should support new wind power development.[15]

One exception to the focus on provincial level policies is the biofuels sector, where Canada has a national minimum requirement of 5 percent renewable content in gasoline and 2 percent in diesel and other distillate heating oil.[16]

Challenges and Barriers to Renewable Energy Exports

Despite Canada ranking as the top market for U.S. renewable energy exports through 2015, export growth is expected to be tempered somewhat by strong local content requirements and the presence of foreign-flagged manufacturers in the market.

Québec has the most stringent local content requirements for renewable energy in Canada, stipulating that 60 percent of a project's cost, and 30 percent of wind turbine costs), be spent in the province. Ontario's local content policies were found to be inconsistent with Canada's obligations under World Trade Organization agreements, and while the province has reformed its incentives, it remains to be seen if the market will open substantially to foreign suppliers.

Unfortunately for many U.S. exporters, Canada's manufacturing capacity has grown as a result of the local content requirements (LCR) in these two provinces. Repower and Enercon – two German-based companies – are the only manufacturers to have operations in Québec, and consequently hold all the contracts for wind projects currently under development in the province.[17]

Additionally, the overall impact of Canada's growing fossil fuel industry on U.S. renewable energy exporters remains unclear. ITA expects that renewable energy will face expanded competition for limited financial resources and political support from traditional fossil fuel resources, particularly in Western Canada.

For example, Alberta – Canada's only completely deregulated electricity market – has seen its power demand increase as a result of oil sands development and the decommissioning of fossil fuel plants. Thus, Alberta may be a good candidate for the expanded use of renewable energy. The province has strong wind resources and falling clean energy prices may make the clean energy sector economically competitive with other forms of energy.

Opportunities for U.S. Companies

Wind
To be successful, wind energy exporters will need to bring creative solutions and niche product or services to the market. *Bloomberg New Energy Finance* expects 6.7 GW of new wind capacity to be brought online in Canada by 2015, but thus far, every announced turbine contract has gone to a firm with local manufacturing. Even products that were previously imported, such as nacelles for the wind industry, are likely to be sourced locally in the future.

U.S.-based component suppliers may find some opportunities selling to turbine manufacturers, but in the short-term, exports are likely to be only in the form of services. Environmental impact consultants, financiers, engineers, and control system designers should all find opportunities.

Hydropower
Canada also ranks first on ITA's list of top hydropower export markets. The market is expected to support close to 80 percent of all hydropower exports from the United States through 2015, although it will only account for 7% of the growth in hydropower capacity globally in that time.

In 2012, the Canadian Hydropower Association estimated that the country has 163 GW of untapped hydropower capacity. Currently, there are only 25 GW of hydropower under construction or in advanced planning.[18] The majority of new development is planned for the provinces of Québec, British Columbia, and Labrador and hydropower export promotion activities in the sector should be focused on these locations.

Ethanol

ITA also expects Canada to be the top biofuels market through 2015. In 2013, more than half of all U.S. ethanol exports were shipped to Canada, valued at over $775 million. Given current incentives in Canada at both the national and provincial levels, as well as the ease of cross-border transport via rail, the competitive position of U.S. exporters in Canada should continue.

Canada's federal mandate of 5 percent ethanol blending (7.5 in Saskatchewan and 8.5 percent in Manitoba) is lower than the 10-15 percent blends in the United States, but production levels are not sufficient to meet the expected 2.7 billion liter annual demand.[19]

Solar

Canada ranks first in terms of solar export opportunities through 2015. Although Canada ranks only 14th globally in terms of expected solar installations through 2015, the country's limited manufacturing capacity in the sector may create opportunities for exports of U.S. solar equipment. Ontario, Québec, and British Columbia have developed emerging solar energy clusters that may support additional development into the future.

Upcoming Renewable Energy Trade Events for Exporters interested in Canada:
- **All Energy Expo and Conference**; *April 9-10, 2014* – Toronto, ON
- **Canadian Wind Power Conference (CanWEA)**; *October 27-30, 2014* – Montreal, QC

U.S. Foreign Commercial Service Contact Information:
Connie Irrera
Commercial Specialist
Email: connie.irrera@trade.gov
Tel: 514-908-3662

For more information, please visit: www.export.gov/reee or www.export.gov/canada.

This page intentionally left blank

Chile

Overall Rank: 4

Type: Large Market; Large Market Share

Though a relative newcomer to the global renewable energy market, Chile's clean energy potential has the country poised to become a significant market for U.S. exporters. Chile's open economy combined with its lack of domestic manufacturing capacity for renewable energy goods indicate that should development occur, U.S. exporters will find considerable opportunities. In particular, solar exporters across the supply chain are likely to find opportunities in Chile, as well as small hydropower developers, early-stage geothermal firms, and wind turbine manufacturers.

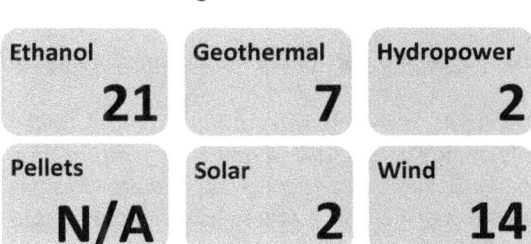

Subsector Rankings

Ethanol	Geothermal	Hydropower
21	7	2

Pellets	Solar	Wind
N/A	2	14

Chile needs to double its energy output in the next 15 years to meet expected demand growth. With almost no fossil fuel resources, the country currently relies on imported electricity to meet its energy needs. Electricity imports have grown dramatically as energy needs have risen – increasing from 42 percent in 1980 to almost 75 percent today.

Most imports are in the form of natural gas from Argentina.[20] Several of Chile's large mining companies, the largest drivers of GDP growth in Chile, have even resorted to imported diesel generation to meet their energy needs, no doubt reducing their profitability. The lack of control over the country's energy supply has led to rising prices and a sense of intense frustration on the part of many Chilean energy consumers.

As a result, the Chilean Government is committed to developing new renewable energy projects and to using off-grid renewable energy technologies to replace existing diesel generation. ITA expects Chile to support exports in every renewable energy power generation sector through 2015; ranking it in the top 10 markets for solar, hydropower, and geothermal exports.

Overview of Renewable Energy Market

Chile enjoys one of the world's strongest resource bases for renewable energy. The Atacama Desert in

Northern Chile is widely considered the world's best solar resource, and similarly strong wind, geothermal, and hydropower resources exist in the country as well. In fact, should Chile develop its full renewable energy potential, it could meet all of its projected energy demand with clean energy generation and have extra power left over to export to neighboring countries.

The Chilean Government has recently begun emphasizing the development of clean energy. A particular emphasis has been placed on low-cost, baseload renewable electricity generation to meet the needs of the mining sector. While the most obvious choice would be new hydropower dams, plans for new dams have been put on hold due to environmental concerns. Instead, concentrated solar power and distributed generation systems have seen tremendous interest, indicating a likelihood of future growth in these sectors.

The Chilean Government passed its first renewable energy law in 2008, creating a national target requiring five percent of Chile's energy to come from non-conventional renewable energy (defined as renewable energy excluding large hydropower above 40 MW) by 2012 – a target set to increase to 10 percent by 2024. Though some political debate occurred in 2011 and 2012 on whether to increase the target to 20 percent by 2020, the President of Chile ultimately decided to reaffirm the lower target in Chile's *National Energy Strategy*, which was released in February 2012.[21] The Strategy is agnostic on the types of renewable energy development it foresees, although most analysts predict that solar energy – despite little development to date – should see the most growth over the coming years.

Challenges and Barriers to Renewable Energy Exports

Despite its tremendous resource potential, Chile has only deployed 880 MW of non-large hydro renewable energy technologies to date. The industry has been slowed considerably by three interrelated factors, all of which must be addressed to facilitate the level of investment needed for Chile to meet its clean energy goals.

First, local financiers have historically been unwilling to invest in renewable energy projects. This is partly a "first-mover" problem, as local banks do not want to take the risk associated with investing in a "new" technology. The situation is aggravated by a frequent unwillingness of utility companies to sign long-term power purchase agreements with developers, making projects risky for investors. This situation appears to be changing quickly, however, as recent projects or acquisitions by First Solar, SunEdison, and Nordex USA, have driven investor interest in the Chilean market.[22]

Second, because Chile's electricity distribution and transmission industry is entirely privatized, the country faces hurdles to incentivizing the development of new grid transmission lines, particularly to remote areas where renewable energy projects are often located. Chilean utility companies who have not dealt with a significant amount of renewable energy before have shown signs of uneasiness about allowing more renewable energy onto their electricity grids. Fortunately, Chile's *National Energy Strategy* identified this issue and called for the expedited construction of additional transmission lines. [23]

Finally, as Chile's economy continues to grow, many citizens have become more closely engaged with efforts to protect the country's tremendous environmental resources, particularly in Southern Chile. As such, several projects – particularly large hydropower projects – have faced considerable public backlash.[24] Small hydropower development has thus become an important topic, as it would help alleviate some of these tensions while also providing baseload electricity to drive additional economic growth.

Opportunities for U.S. Companies

U.S. companies are already well-positioned in Chile due to the existing U.S.-Chile Free Trade Agreement and the strong bilateral commercial relationship between the two countries. As a result, American companies are often welcomed to Chile as they are widely seen as having leading technology and experience developing new products.

Solar
ITA expects the solar industry to account for the vast majority of U.S. renewable energy exports to Chile in the near-term. Though only a small number of solar projects currently exist in Chile (mostly for rural electrification purposes), a pipeline of over 3 GW of new projects should drive export growth going forward. With no current solar manufacturing capacity, all of Chile's solar development will be met by imports in the short-term; thereby explaining one of the reasons why ITA ranked Chile among its top solar exports markets.

ITA believes that solar projects, built to support Chile's mining operations in the North, provide an important opportunity to catalyze the Chilean market into the future. A recently announced 100 MW solar project developed by SunEdison for CAP, a large mining company, is a perfect example. The project, partially funded by OPIC, will be the largest solar project in Latin America, and should allow Chilean decision-makers – i.e., other mine operators, Chilean bankers, and other industrial consumers – to see firsthand the benefits of solar energy, making future investments in the sector more likely.

It will be important for solar exporters to keep Chilean decision-makers aware of both the latest U.S.-developed solar technologies and of the expected price declines of solar products. While investor interest is certainly increasing, solar exporters must demonstrate the ability of solar technologies to meet the specific needs of Chilean consumers, particularly those of mining companies. This will likely require an effort to develop energy storage alongside solar installations to provide continuous power to mining operations.

Wind
Although Chile did not commission any new wind projects in 2012, 530 MW of wind projects have secured financing and are expected to come online in the near-term. Several firms have also purchased operational or close-to-operational wind projects in

Chile with the intent of updating or outfitting the project with their own technology.

Hydropower

ITA expects small- to medium-sized hydropower companies to find opportunities for developing projects in the short-term. Chile ranks behind only Canada in terms of projected U.S. hydropower exports through 2015. Run-of-river hydropower projects in low-flow areas like irrigation and already constructed navigational dams should provide the most export opportunities.

Geothermal

Despite its vast geothermal potential, to date no geothermal projects have been commissioned in Chile or anywhere else in South America. A 2012 tender generated $250 million in investments for 20 geothermal energy exploration concessions. The concessions have a two-year expiration date, which ITA believes will jump-start the geothermal market and push Chile to seventh place on ITA's list of top geothermal export markets through 2015.

Most of Chile's geothermal development will be brought online in the 2016-2020 timeframe.[25] Since geothermal purchasing decisions are often made 1-3 years prior to a project coming online, many of these projects could provide important export opportunities for U.S. companies in the near-term.

Upcoming Renewable Energy Trade Events for Exporters interested in Chile:
- **IFT Energy & Water 2014**; *July 22-24, 2014* – Antofagasta, Chile

U.S. Foreign Commercial Service Contact Information: Marcelo Orellana
Commercial Specialist
Email: Marcelo.Orellana@trade.gov
Tel: (56-2) 2330-3455

For more information, please visit: www.export.gov/reee or www.export.gov/chile.

This page intentionally left blank

China
Overall Rank: **2**

Type: Large Market; Small Market Share

While China remains a frustrating market with considerable barriers, the sheer size of its renewable energy market presents unprecedented opportunities for U.S. exporters. In fact, despite a noted lack of market share, China ranks #2 on ITA's list of top renewable energy export markets through 2015 despite several ongoing competitiveness challenges, including insufficient intellectual property rights enforcement and a strong predilection to purchase technology at the lowest possible cost regardless of quality. While some U.S. exporters can find enormous success in China, others are confronted with extensive barriers and disappointment.

Sub-Sector Rankings

Ethanol	Geothermal	Hydropower
28	18	11

Pellets	Solar	Wind
13	4	1

China is both the world's largest supplier of and the largest market for renewable energy technologies. Over the next two decades, it will install more wind, solar, and hydropower capacity than any other country. As such it will remain a critical market for U.S. exporters well into the future. Yet despite considerable market growth, the Chinese renewable energy market can be difficult for American exporters to enter successfully.

The complexity of the Chinese market and a general lack of market share enjoyed by U.S.-based firms often makes doing business in China difficult. While the market has supported several export deals in the past, including turning previously small companies into global players, it is also characterized by a large number of firms that were rendered unsuccessful due to intellectual property infringements.

American exporters are encouraged to be constantly mindful of threats to their intellectual property, hire local counsel, if necessary, and develop China-specific strategies for market entry that are consistent with the threat level associated with their intellectual property.

Overview of the Renewable Energy Market

Encouraging renewable energy generation has been a priority for China since the 12th Five-Year Plan was announced in 2010. The plan created a number of

ambitious targets, including 100 GW of grid-connected wind capacity and 21 GW of solar capacity by 2015. In early 2013, the solar capacity target was revised upwards to 35GW to boost domestic adoption and aid China's solar industry. The plan also called for 420 GW of hydropower and 200 GW of wind, 50 GW of solar and 30 GW of biomass and waste-to-energy by 2020 – some of the highest targets in the world. In 2013, China's National Energy Administration reaffirmed these targets, announcing that China was on pace to meet or exceed each mandate.[26]

To ensure its goals are met, China has implemented a variety of policy tools. Competitive auctions have been utilized to decide power tariffs for wind and solar projects (onshore wind and solar PV have since been removed from this system). Feed-in-tariffs (FIT) have been developed for onshore wind, biomass and waste-to-energy, and solar PV projects.

And through the 2009 Golden Sun Program, China has offered capex subsidies for residential solar installations, driving the rooftop PV market. On Oct 29, 2013, China's National Energy Administration issued a "solicitation letter of photovoltaic power construction scale in 2013 and 2014" that requests the total PV installation capacity to reach 12GW in 2014, including 8 GW of distributed PV projects and 4GW of utility-scale projects.

China is also considering a renewable energy quota system similar to a renewable energy portfolio standard. The system would create renewable energy targets for the top 14 power companies in China (representing two-thirds of the market) and the four grid operators. If such a program is implemented, identifying opportunities to engage these firms will be important for U.S. renewable energy exporters, as these could be captive buyers of clean energy technologies for the foreseeable future.

Challenges and Barriers to Renewable Energy Exports

Despite the growth expected in China's renewable energy market, U.S. exporters face several important challenges that limit U.S. competitiveness. First, China is still recovering from vast oversupply in its wind and solar markets (the size of its domestic manufacturing base has contributed substantially to the oversupply of these technologies globally). As a result, Chinese industry has entered a period of intense restructuring. Suntech, the largest Chinese solar company, filed for bankruptcy in March 2013 despite receiving billions in direct loans from the Chinese Government. ITA expects mergers and acquisitions within China to continue over the next few years, as demand for products slowly reaches the availability of supply.

To counter the oversupply of wind and solar capacity, China has moved forcefully to promote domestic consumption and to protect its domestic manufacturers from foreign competition, causing trade tensions to rise in Europe and the United States.[27] The litigious environment created by these cases has further clouded the ability of U.S. suppliers to do business in China.

Additionally, the lack of sufficient protection and enforcement of intellectual property rights in China remains a consistent barrier for many U.S. exporters. U.S. companies, especially small- and medium-sized firms, should be cautious when exporting to China, ensuring that they have the proper legal protections and strategy in place before entering the market.

In the renewable fuels industry, China restricts ethanol imports for fuel and maintains state ownership over its existing ethanol plants. As a result, China ranks only 28th on ITA's list of top ethanol export markets through 2015 and exporters are encouraged to look elsewhere for more attractive opportunities.

Opportunities for U.S. Companies

Despite relatively high transportation costs, U.S. companies continue to have success exporting high value-added products. As products become increasingly commoditized, the opportunity to export from the United States decreases exponentially.[28] Companies that offer niche services like grid reliability, engineering, or environmental consultancy may find some opportunities in emerging locations (i.e., second or third-tier cities) where U.S. products and services may face less direct competition from Chinese suppliers.

Solar
China already stands as the largest producer of solar technologies and is quickly becoming the largest consumer as well. The surge in local demand has been facilitated by the Chinese Government and has left very few opportunities for U.S. exporters relative to the market as a whole. Under the Golden Sun Program, for example, the Government not only provided incentives to consumers, but also selected the module supplier through a centralized process in which no U.S. supplier has ever won a contract.

Despite ranking China fourth in terms of overall solar exports, exports in the sector will be the result of sheer volume – not on the relative competitive position of U.S. exporters. Companies are encouraged to consider whether China is the right market for them, as other markets may be easier to enter and hold the potential for stronger export competitiveness.

Wind
No market is expected to support as many wind exports as China. China's vast market and an unprecedented investment in the sector should support considerable exports from the United States, even in spite of very little U.S. market share. As China shifts its focus to small- and medium-sized wind farms, increased technical and safety standards, and newer technologies, the demand for innovative products and technical components may provide new opportunities for U.S. companies.[29] Many older Chinese wind farms, for example, are facing low capacity factors and frequent operational problems. Demand for higher-efficiency retrofits will likely increase as a result.[30]

Hydropower
China has the largest hydropower resource in the world and the largest pipeline of projects, totaling 80 GW of expected capacity.[31] U.S. exporters may find opportunities in the design, engineering, and

development of hydropower projects in China. U.S. engineering and construction firms are often globally competitive and these services account for a large portion of a hydropower project's costs. Nevertheless, according to ITA's analysis, China will account for less than 1 percent of total hydropower exports through 2015. Almost the entire Chinese market will be captured by Chinese firms.

Biomass
ITA anticipates a further increase in demand for biogas recovery and utilization technologies, creating a potential export opportunity for U.S. firms with anaerobic digester or gas purification technology.[32] China has set ambitious targets for biomass production, including 2 GW of biogas installed capacity and 3 GW of waste-to-energy by 2015. Additionally, there are signs that China is interested in transitioning some of its coal-fired power plants towards biomass co-firing – all of which should create some opportunity for U.S. feedstock exporters in the near-term.

Upcoming Renewable Energy Trade Events for Exporters interested in China:
- **Solarcon 2014**; *March 18-20, 2014* – Shanghai
- **Wind Power China 2014**; *October 26-28, 2014* – Beijing

For more information, please visit www.export.gov/reee or www.export.gov/china.

This page intentionally left blank

India

Overall Rank: **15**

Type: Large Market; Small Market Share

The Indian renewable energy market remains one of the most challenging and unwelcoming markets for American exporters globally. Strong local content requirements and a complicated business climate make export deals difficult. Exporters are encouraged to consider state-level projects and to find niche opportunities, particularly in the export of renewable energy related services.

Sub-Sector Rankings

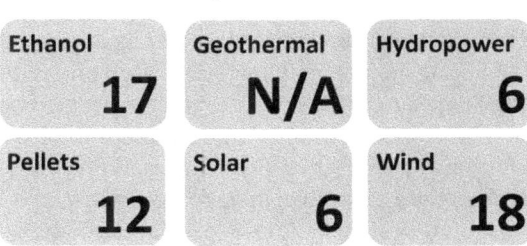

Ethanol	Geothermal	Hydropower
17	N/A	6

Pellets	Solar	Wind
12	6	18

India is already one of the world's largest energy markets and growth is expected to continue relatively unabated into the future. In 2012, India added 23.6 GW of new power generation – more than the entire installed capacity of several medium-sized countries.

Yet India faces significant energy challenges, including a vast gap between energy supply and demand, a large population that still lacks access to regular electricity, and the need to limit carbon emissions; challenges that, if overcome, would enable more sustainable economic growth well into the future.

Two factors in particular underpin almost every energy decision. First, India needs more power. Rolling brownouts have hampered economic growth and limited foreign investment in the country. The July 2012 blackout that affected 620 million, for example, was seen globally as an embarrassment that needed to be corrected.[33]

Second, India fervently wants to be a clean energy leader – not just as a consumer of clean energy products, but as a producer. As a result, the Indian government is unlikely to change course in the face of international pressure to open its renewable energy market to foreign imports, and export opportunities may be limited going forward as more local production comes online.

Overview of the Renewable Energy Market

Renewable energy accounted for roughly 12 percent of India's power production during the first months of 2013.[34] Large hydropower accounts for the vast majority of India's renewable energy capacity, reaching over 39 GW by the end of March 2013. Wind power accounts for the next largest installed capacity (20 GW), followed by small hydropower (4.8 GW).[35]

The solar sector is expected to grow significantly from just over 340 MW at the end of 2011 to over 7 GW by 2015.[36] The growth is supported at the national level by the Jawaharlal Nehru National Solar Mission (JNNSM), which was launched in 2009 and called for 20 GW of new solar capacity by 2022. The JNNSM has been implemented by the Indian Ministry of New and Renewable Energy, which allocates projects through an auction to developers who offer to supply power at the lowest rate possible.

Challenges and Barriers to Renewable Energy Exports

Unfortunately for U.S. exporters, the JNNSM includes strong LCRs that significantly reduce the export potential provided by the Indian market. Phase 1 of the JNNSM banned the import of crystalline-silicon solar cells (the ban was later extended to include modules). Phase 2 of the JNNSM, which was announced in early 2013, includes a similar commitment to local content.

The first solar auction under Phase II, announced in October 2013, reserved 375 MW of the 750 MW auction for developers who committed to using only Indian-made equipment.[37]

In addition to an obstructive policy environment, U.S. exporters face several structural barriers that make U.S. exports relatively uncompetitive. For example, the cost of financing in the Indian market is often prohibitively high. For solar projects, the cost of borrowing money can be 13-14 percent.[38] Partly as a result of the cost of financing and partly because other markets have become more attractive, India's clean energy investment peaked in 2011 and is not expected to reach similar levels going forward.[39] Most renewable energy technologies cost less than they did in 2011, so development should continue unabated, but investor interest has waned.

Exporters are therefore advised to consider India as an export destination only if the market fits well into a company's specific export strategy. Other markets are simply larger, more attractive, and easier to navigate. If exporters are interested in the Indian market, they are highly encouraged to contact the Foreign Commercial Service in India for details on market entry and recent policy announcements.

Opportunities for U.S. Companies

Wind
Annual wind installations in India are set to decline for the second straight year as a lack of policy certainty has slowed investment in the sector. To address this, the Indian government announced in March 2013 that it will renew generation-based incentives for wind energy, although details of the structure were not disclosed. Based on the previous incentive, *Bloomberg New Energy Finance* (BNEF) predicts India should install roughly 5 GW of new wind projects in 2014.[40]

Importantly, independent power producers have continued to show faith in the long-term value of the Indian wind market, as they continue to announce new projects. Some projects have already secured financing, but lenders appear less positive on the market and often seem reluctant to move quickly.

Despite projected growth, American wind companies remain at a severe disadvantage in India due to the dominance that local turbine manufacturers have in the market. The top four wind developers in India are all Indian companies. Wind World India, the former Indian

subsidiary of German firm Enercon, which severed ties with its German parent in January 2013, recently overtook Suzlon as the market leader for the first time in more than a decade. ReGen Powertech and Inox Wind are the third and fourth largest developers.[41]

Due to the challenges, India ranks only 18th in terms of projected U.S. exports through 2015. U.S. exporters may find some opportunities in exporting component parts and services, especially because India does not charge an import duty for wind turbine components.

Solar
ITA expects India to install more solar energy capacity through 2015 than any country except Japan and China. Despite severe local content requirements in projects that receive incentives from the JNNSM, the sheer size of the limited slices of the market open to international businesses is large enough to rank India sixth on ITA's list of top solar export markets through 2015.

Some exporters have previously found success using Ex-Im Bank financing, but given the restructured local content provisions under Phase II of India's National Solar Mission, those opportunities may be ending. As a result, ITA encourages solar exporters to consider projects developed through state-level incentives, which often do not mandate the use of local content. According to Phase II draft guidelines, state programs should account for 5.4 GW of new development to 2017, with only 3.6 GW allocated through national-level auctions.[42]

Currently three states – Gujarat, Rajasthan, and Maharashtra – account for 90 percent of India's total solar capacity, but other states have begun to enter the market as well. In 2013, Tamil Nadu, Andhra Pradesh, Karnataka, Punjab, and Uttar Pradesh all offered solar auctions. Many of these auctions were unsuccessful in contracting their targeted amount of capacity, however, as too many auctions in a short period of time and weak power purchase agreements caused developer interest to wane.

Ethanol
The situation for ethanol exports is evolving quickly in India with consequences for the competitiveness of U.S. exporters. While the Indian Government's previous policy focused on domestic production, in April 2013 it was reported that Indian companies were experiencing a shortfall of domestic ethanol to comply with India's five percent blend mandate. Indian companies scrambled to obtain foreign ethanol with one company

seeking 820 million liters of ethanol from international suppliers.[43] The resulting demand for international ethanol caused prices to rise, the backlash of which was a threat from the Indian government to impose price controls for imported ethanol. If such a price control was implemented, export opportunities may be short lived.[44]

Biomass

U.S. exporters may also find opportunities in the biomass and waste-to-energy sectors, although at a much smaller scale than either solar or wind. MNRE announced that it will likely increase funding for waste-to-energy projects in order to meet India's goal of 4 GW of installed capacity by the end of the 12th Five Year Plan in 2017, but details have yet to follow.

Hydropower

India ranks sixth on ITA's list of top hydropower export markets through 2015 thanks to its well-developed market and significant growth potential. India has over 39 GW of installed hydropower capacity currently online, but 50 GW of projects are currently under development. The Northeast states of Assam and Arunachal Pradesh have a majority of the undeveloped hydropower potential.

As in other renewable energy sectors in India, project development can be slowed down by bureaucratic red tape, leaving potential U.S. exports waiting for approvals from the Indian Government. Project delays are common, with development times from 10 to 15 years on large-scale hydropower projects. Nevertheless, exports of U.S. expertise and small hydropower technologies are likely in the near-term.

Upcoming Renewable Energy Trade Events for Exporters interested in India:
- **Renewable Energy India**; *September 3-5, 2014* – New Delhi

U.S. Foreign Commercial Service Contact Information: Renie Subin
Commercial Specialist
Email: Renie.Subin@trade.gov
Tel: 91-11-2331 6841thru 49 ext.2155

For more information, please visit: www.export.gov/reee or www.export.gov/india.

This page intentionally left blank

Italy

Overall Rank: **25**

Type: Large Market; Small Market Share

Italy is currently the world's second largest producer of solar energy behind Germany. Though future installations are expected to lag behind those in other markets, the country offers both unmet potential and supportive government policies that should drive investment in renewable energies for the foreseeable future. U.S. exporters, however, face fierce competition from European- and Asian-based suppliers. Exporters must fully understand Italy's changing policy regime to identify niche opportunities.

Sub-Sector Rankings

Ethanol	Geothermal	Hydropower
N/A	17	31

Pellets	Solar	Wind
6	10	26

Exporters are often surprised to learn that Italy is one of the world's most important renewable energy markets. It has a well-diversified renewable energy project base, including significant development to date in the solar, wind, hydropower, geothermal, and biomass industries. By the end of 2012, Italy had installed 16.3GW of solar power (more than any country except Germany), 8.1 GW of wind power, 1.9 GW of biomass, and 882 MW of geothermal energy.[45]

ITA expects solar power to account for the most exports to Italy in the short-term, as most new renewable energy investment is expected to focus on solar development. In fact, ITA anticipates that Italy will install the fifth most solar capacity globally through 2015. Though the market will be considerably smaller than the solar market in China, Japan, and India, it is expected to provide significant export opportunities across a variety of solar subsectors.

Overview of the Renewable Energy Market

A generous Feed-in-Tariff (FIT) regime and renewable portfolio standards have driven Italy's renewable energy market since 2005. In 2009, the Italian Government committed to obtaining 17 percent of the country's electricity from renewable sources by 2020.[46] However, due to the rapid adoption of technologies like wind and solar, the share of renewables in Italy's electricity mix

reached 28 percent in 2012, nearly a decade ahead of Italy's stated goals.[47]

Since the Government launched incentives eight years ago, more than 526,000 solar installations have been completed, including several large utility-scale PV projects in southern Italy.[48] Northern urban areas conversely have witnessed a boom in roof-mounted systems.

Yet the incentives proved costly to the Government. In response to rising costs and economy-wide fiscal challenges, Italy introduced a degression mechanism for reducing FIT rates in 2012, as well as an overall cap on spending and a registry system to control future capacity installations.[49]

Feed-in premiums replaced fixed tariffs for larger PV projects in June 2013. Shortly thereafter, Italy's national grid operator, GSE, announced that FIT spending to support solar development had reached Italy's cap of €6.7 billion. As a result, there is currently no FIT scheme in place to support new solar PV installations, but installers of PV panels can still benefit from tax deductions for renovation works and from Italy's "net metering" scheme. FITs, green certificates and other types of incentives still apply to other renewable energy sources.

In total, the new incentive mix is expected to be successful, albeit less so than the previous policy regime. Estimates indicate that roughly 3.5 GW of new solar power, 2 GW of new wind power (both onshore and offshore), and 990 MW of new biomass development will be installed through 2015.[50]

Challenges and Barriers to Renewable Energy Exports

The new incentive program includes a differentiated FIT scheme for different technologies and project sizes. Non-solar PV renewable energy projects over 1 MW, for example, qualify for a base rate plus a premium for the specific technology used in the project. The base tariff is determined based on bids in a tendering process, but must be derived between six size classes and two separate applications (rooftop and all others).[51]

Additionally, all but the smallest renewable energy projects must now apply to a national registry that tracks incentives and installed capacity to ensure that each project is assigned the premium incentive it deserves. Incentives for each technology will be capped on an annual basis.[52]

For many developers, the new incentives add considerable complexity to the market, which in the short-term is expected to slow investment as financiers decipher how best to move forward. The uncertainty, however, presents an opportunity for many American firms that have expertise navigating the complex policy environment in the United States, particularly financial services firms and legal experts.

An additional obstacle to U.S. renewable energy exports is the strong competition from European firms and lower cost Asian suppliers. European-based companies naturally face lower transportation costs, often putting U.S. suppliers at a price disadvantage. For large or commoditized products, exports are thus largely unlikely due to transportation costs. But, more easily transported products like solar cells, modules, and biomass feedstocks can find opportunities – as can new or innovative products that have not been deployed at scale in Italy to date.

Opportunities for U.S. Companies

Italy's renewable energy project pipeline remains deep and relatively well funded despite recent policy changes that some analysts have suggested could slowly withdraw investment capital from the market. As a result, ITA expects export opportunities to remain –

although American companies are not expected to see any new competitive advantages through 2015, making exports difficult.

Solar
In the short-term, Italy's new policy incentives are expected to support smaller, distributed generation systems. Almost all of the newly permitted solar installations will be systems under 200 kW and be used in residential and commercial settings.[53] These kinds of systems are already well developed in the United States and should provide U.S. exporters some comparative advantage, particularly those firms with experience leasing solar equipment.

Exporters of solar modules for utility-scale projects will likely find larger opportunities elsewhere, as most products for this market segment will often be sourced either from Europe or lower-cost suppliers from Asia.

Wind
Wind energy is the second-most installed renewable energy technology in Italy, with a cumulative installed capacity of 8.1 GW.[54] U.S. wind energy exporters, facing stiff competition from European suppliers, will likely need to offer wind turbine component parts, or a niche product where they have a competitive advantage. For example, Northern Power, a small wind company based in Vermont used Ex-Im financing to facilitate the sale of 55 of its 100 kW wind turbines for FIT projects in Italy. Finding similar projects and utilizing Ex-Im financing could lead to additional exports for American companies.

Most Italian wind developers will likely source turbines, towers, and other large equipment from local or regional manufacturers located elsewhere in the European Union. Nevertheless, exporters of services associated with these products may find some opportunities, although exports are expected to be limited.

Biomass
Italy ranks sixth on ITA's list of top biomass pellet markets for U.S. exporters in the near-term. The first auction under the new premium FIT program in January 2013 saw biomass quotas fully subscribed, indicating a pipeline of projects that should support U.S. exports in the short-term.[55] According to *Bloomberg New Energy Finance*, 123 MW of new biomass or waste-to-energy projects have been announced in Italy. If these projects are ultimately developed, U.S.-based technology and

expertise should be well positioned in the market to support export sales.[56]

Geothermal

There are currently no new geothermal facilities planned in Italy. Yet interest in geothermal energy appears to be growing, and given the United States' competitive position in the industry, early stage geothermal development assistance, like resource mapping, could entice enough Italian interest in the sector that investment and development may follow.[57]

Upcoming Renewable Energy Trade Events for Exporters interested in Italy:
- **Mostra Convegno Expocomfort**; *March 18-21, 2014* – Milan
- **Solarexpo**; *May 7-9, 2014* – Milan
- **Ecomondo**; *November 5-8, 2014* – Rimini

U.S. Foreign Commercial Service Contact Information: Federico Bevini
Industry Sector Specialist
Email: federico.bevini@trade.gov
Tel: +39 02 626 88 520

For more information, please visit: www.export.gov/reee or www.export.gov/italy.

This page intentionally left blank

Japan

Overall Rank: **17**

Type: Large Market; Small Market Share

The introduction of a feed-in-tariff (FIT) has attracted significant investment in the Japanese renewable energy market, particularly in the solar sector where demand for products outpaces Japan's domestic production capacity. Japan has traditionally been a difficult market for American renewable energy exporters to compete, with few American firms enjoying significant market share. In the short-term, however, unprecedented growth as a result of new incentives may create opportunities for U.S. firms, particularly when partnered with a strong domestic distributor or investor.

Sub-Sector Rankings

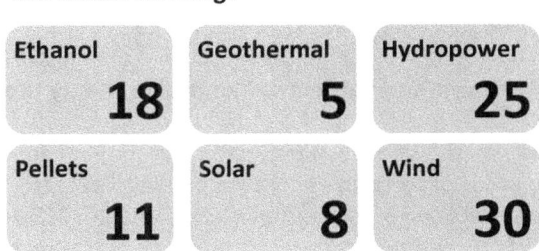

Ethanol	Geothermal	Hydropower
18	**5**	**25**

Pellets	Solar	Wind
11	**8**	**30**

The Japanese renewable energy market is both large and widespread, encompassing multiple renewable energy subsectors. Yet the market has historically attracted little foreign competition, as many Japanese decision-makers have shown a strong preference for buying products from domestic companies.

The lack of investment has been punctuated by the presence of 10 vertically-integrated electric power companies, which has created challenges for the Japanese government. As newly installed renewable energy comes online and energy demand continues to grow, the government must facilitate the creation of an electricity system that can continue to meet the needs of Japanese citizens. Following Japan's retreat from civil nuclear in the aftermath of the March 2011 earthquake, tsunami, and subsequent failure of the Fukushima Daiichi nuclear power plant, the challenges became even more severe, presenting a unique opportunity for American renewable energy exporters in Japan.

Japan had supported renewable energy development since 2005, but moved quickly after the disaster to bolster its previous national targets and spur heightened renewable energy investment. A feed-in-tariff (FIT) regime was launched that received significant international attention. In line with its aim for 28 GW of solar energy to be installed by 2020, Japan's FIT rate for solar was particularly attractive. Almost immediately

investors, developers, and component manufacturers flocked to the market, making Japan one of the most exciting and dynamic renewable energy markets globally.

Despite this, renewable energy still only accounted for 9 percent of electricity generation in 2012 (with non-hydro sources at only 1.6%). With most nuclear power offline, the urgent need was immediately filled with increased oil and liquefied natural gas imports (16 and 48 percent, respectively).[58] The Japanese government is also under pressure from the business community to restore nuclear power. The draft revised energy plan released by METI in December 2013 acknowledged that an unspecified amount of nuclear power would inevitably be part of the nation's energy mix.

Overview of the Renewable Energy Market

In the year following the introduction of the FIT, Japan approved a rapid 3.3 GW of new renewable energy capacity.[59] The vast majority of this project pipeline was in the solar sector, but wind, biomass, and geothermal projects were also approved. In fact, despite an almost 10 percent reduction in the solar FIT in April 2013, the current roughly 38 yen per kWh rate is still attractive to investors and developers.[60] The FIT for wind, hydro, biomass, and geothermal electricity production remained unchanged.

A Ministry of Economy, Trade, and Industry (METI) committee will start meeting in January 2014 to consider changes to the various FIT rates to be announced in April 2014. Dramatic reductions are not expected; and some reports even predict new FIT categories, such as off-shore wind. As such, ITA projects Japan to continue to be one of the most dynamic renewable energy markets through 2015.

Challenges and Barriers to Renewable Energy Exports

Despite the significant projected investment expected to occur, Japan ranks only 17th on ITA's list of top renewable energy export markets through 2015 due to stiff competition and a traditional lack of U.S. market share.

Although Japan's ability to attract international renewable energy investment remains strong, questions persist as to whether all of its approved projects will be fully commissioned. Only 10 percent of approved solar projects have been fully commissioned to date, as a result of difficulties in obtaining financing, land zoning issues, and many developers' anticipation that component prices will continue to fall.

Moreover, development has also been slowed by complications in reaching grid connection agreements with Japanese electric utilities. Japan's utilities have the right to reject FIT approved projects if connecting the new renewable supply interferes with stability of the utility's electricity supply.[61] There are threats from some utilities to curtail renewables or deny access to their transmission grids, due to the variability that such a large increase in renewable energy capacity creates.[62]

For instance, Hokkaido Electric Power Company (HEPCO) has already rejected connection agreements and curtailed the amount of solar electricity it will accept. METI is working with HEPCO to install "smart" batteries that will allow the utility to accept more renewable energy connections, perhaps offering an opportunity for U.S. energy storage firms. Okinawa Electric Power Company is facing similar challenges.

In the solar industry, exports of U.S.-made modules face two additional challenges. First, intense competition from lower cost suppliers elsewhere in Asia has limited the share of the market captured by U.S. exporters. Chinese and Korean firms have captured a large share of the Japanese import market since the new incentives were announced, limiting opportunities for U.S. suppliers. And second, many Japanese firms that

produce technology abroad have begun shipping products back to Japan from their facilities elsewhere around the world. Sharp and Kyocera, for example, now "export" solar products from Mexico and Eastern Europe back to Japan. These cells were originally meant for the U.S. and European markets, but have been redirected to meet orders in Japan.[63]

Opportunities for U.S. Companies

The sheer size of Japan's renewable energy expansion, and the investment opportunity it has created, should provide opportunities for U.S. exporters capable of providing cutting-edge technologies and services to the market. Capturing opportunities in the Japanese market, however, can be difficult. U.S. companies typically need a Japanese partner capable of identifying upcoming projects, conducting face-to-face meetings in Japanese, facilitating import procedures and delivery, and providing after-sales service. Additionally, ITA strongly advises renewable energy exporters to foster relationships with Japan's regional utilities, along with their major contractors and suppliers.

Solar
Despite the challenges, Japan's estimated solar market of nearly 17 GW through 2015 — more than any other country except China — makes it a critically important opportunity for American exporters. The market has traditionally been largely residential, but that is changing. Over 90 percent of approved solar projects in the first year of the FIT program were larger than 10 kW (indicating utility-scale projects).

There has consequently been a shift in the types of solar panels demanded by Japanese consumers. Higher priced, higher efficiency multicrystalline silicon modules are no longer the preferred solar technology in Japan. Instead, cheaper multicrystalline silicon modules are now more attractive, as these panels are more likely to be used in larger projects.[64] This should create an opportunity for U.S. exporters, particularly thin film module manufacturers, who can offer lower costs to project developers.

The potentially lucrative residential solar module market, which has been dominated by either Japanese manufacturers or cheap Asian imports, is a difficult niche for U.S. suppliers. In addition, navigating the testing and certification requirements that are unique to Japan takes patience and financial commitment.

Biomass

While not as large as the solar opportunity in Japan, U.S. exporters of biomass pellets may also find considerable opportunities. According to *Bloomberg New Energy Finance,* through February 2013, Japan approved 27 new biomass projects totaling 147 MW under the FIT program. Most of the projects were announced by paper and lumber manufacturers.[65] Because Japanese feedstock prices are higher than the global average, exports to Japan could be attractive to American pellet manufacturers, although competition from other international sources, such as Canada, remains fierce.

Ethanol

Japan produces only enough biofuels to meet 10 percent of its biofuels demand, with imports expected to account for the difference.[66] Currently Thailand dominates the Asian ethanol market, but U.S. ethanol is cost competitive. In April 2013 – when the government extended the tax credit for gasoline blended with at least 3 percent bioethanol through March 2018 – future demand was given an important boost. Generally speaking, however, Japanese government policies favor electric vehicles over ethanol as a clean energy solution for transportation.

Geothermal

Estimates indicate that Japan ranks third in the world behind the United States and Indonesia in terms of geothermal resource potential, enjoying 15.7 GW of geothermal potential.[67] Due to permitting and land use issues (most of the best geothermal spots are near national parks), only 537 MW, or 3 percent of this potential has been developed. Japan's need to produce baseload power suggests that this resource can no longer be ignored. Japan may begin to revise its environmental regulations in the next several years to enable greater use of its geothermal resources.

Testifying to its recognition of this need, the Japanese government has allocated $126 million for the surveying of geothermal resources in Fiscal Year 2013. While no large projects will be constructed through 2015, exports of equipment and services may be possible in the surveying, exploratory drilling, and resource assessment.[68] These are areas in which U.S. companies already excel. Additionally, some U.S developers are finding success by working with hot springs resorts and local municipalities with geothermal assets. These small-scale production facilities provide local power as well as sell excess electricity back to utilities.

Hydropower

Japan's hydropower market is expected to be limited through 2015 with only modest growth and export potential expected. Small hydro FIT rates did facilitate the approval of several small hydropower projects totaling 27.9 MW.[69] As these projects are developed, U.S. firms may find some opportunities exporting hydropower services, like environmental assessment consulting or engineering expertise. Most hydro products are expected to be procured locally.[70]

Wind

ITA expects the Japanese government's next renewable energy policy push to be in the wind energy sector. Indeed, METI has already estimated the cost of enhancing the Japanese electricity grid in Hokkaido and Tohoku in an effort to support future wind development. According to some plans, METI will develop a cost-bearing scheme called a Special-Purpose Corporation (SPC) to invest in new grid construction. The SPC would be half financed by a wind power generation company. Local utilities would then pay the SPC for the use of the new grid infrastructure. Additionally, METI is considering adding a new offshore wind FIT in the next round of FIT adjustments in March 2014. Press reports indicate this will be the most lucrative FIT.

Unfortunately, U.S. exports in the wind sector are expected to be limited to niche markets like small-scale wind power, as the United States enjoys very little market share in Japan.

Upcoming Renewable Energy Trade Events for Exporters interested in Japan:
- **World Smart Energy Week Japan (Certified Trade Fair)**; *February 26-28, 2014 –* Tokyo Big Sight, Tokyo
- **New Orleans Association Conference**; *May 22, 2014 –* Tokyo
- **Smart Community Japan**; *June 18-20, 2014 –* Tokyo Big Sight, Tokyo
- **Grand Renewable Energy 2014 International Conference and Exhibition**; *July 27-August 1, 2014 -* Tokyo Big Sight, Tokyo
- **PV Japan**; *July 30-August 1, 2014 -* Tokyo Big Sight, Tokyo
- **U.S. Japan Renewable Energy Policy Business Roundtable**; *December 2014*

U.S. Foreign Commercial Service Contact Information: Misa Shimizu
Commercial Specialist
Email: Misa.Shimizu@trade.gov
Tel: 81-3-3224-5076

For more information, please visit: www.export.gov/reee or www.export.gov/japan.

Mexico

Overall Rank: **5**

Type: Small Market; Large Market Share

Perhaps no market offers as much potential for future U.S. renewable energy exports as Mexico. Mexico's proximity to the United States and its resource potential portend significant U.S. exports, but the market is currently small and growth is difficult to project given the ongoing energy reform efforts of President Peña Nieto. As implementing regulations are approved, exporters are encouraged to further develop their contacts in Mexico and position themselves for opportunities should new renewable energy investment begin to materialize.

Sub-Sector Rankings

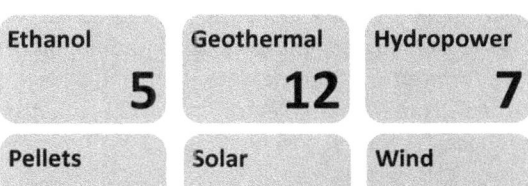

Ethanol	Geothermal	Hydropower
5	12	7

Pellets	Solar	Wind
10	18	3

Mexico is already a key destination for U.S. renewable energy exports. The close relationship between many U.S-based suppliers and their Mexican counterparts, as well as the interlinked nature of supply chains in both countries, has facilitated several export deals despite only modest investment in the sector compared to other markets. As a result, ITA ranks Mexico #5 on its list of top renewable energy export destinations through 2015, with opportunities projected in every renewable energy subsector.

Yet while exports are likely in a "business-as-usual" climate, ongoing energy reform efforts offer the potential to dramatically increase investment in the renewable energy sector, potentially creating even more opportunities in the near-to-medium term. Exporters are highly encouraged to monitor the development of implementing regulations for the reform package that passed in December 2013, keeping in mind that any change in incentives or procedures could generate new business opportunities.

Overview of the Renewable Energy Market

Mexico's current renewable energy market is shaped by its "General Law on Climate Change," which was enacted in June 2012. The law affirmed Mexico's intent to increase its electricity generated from clean energy

sources, including nuclear energy, to 35 percent by 2024. International investment in Mexico's renewable energy market increased sharply as a result of the legislation, rising from just $532 million in 2011 to $2.9 billion in 2012.

Most of the renewable energy investment in Mexico has historically supported the wind industry, but other sectors have benefited as well from opportunities created by the law. In fact, Mexico generated 28 percent more renewable energy in 2012 than the year prior, surpassing 12,000 GWh for the first time, and future growth is highly anticipated.

Based on language in the recent energy reform package, Mexico's renewable energy market is expected to be strengthened – but only slightly. The reform bill is largely focused on PEMEX, Mexico's state-run oil company, and is designed to facilitate foreign investment in unconventional oil and gas development, but some changes to electricity regulations could support new renewable energy development as well. As in any reform effort, early adopters to the reform regulations will likely capture new opportunities ahead of other competitors.

Challenges and Barriers to Renewable Energy Exports

The vertically-integrated, single-buyer electricity market model historically used in Mexico has often made the Mexican regulatory framework difficult to navigate for many U.S. companies. Until the recent reform, most of the negotiating power was in the hands of the government and, as a result, prices offered to renewable energy developers were traditionally below prices offered in other markets.[71] In fact, by law, Mexico's state-owned electric utility, CFE, must still purchase the lowest cost electricity.

Squaring this mandate with Mexico's target to increase its share of clean energy generation to 35 percent by 2024 is exceedingly difficult. As a result, CRE, the Mexican energy regulator, has allowed renewable energy developers to file for a "self-supply" contract, meaning that individual consumers – mostly large industrial companies – can produce their own power somewhere in Mexico and then take an equal amount of power off the grid for their own use.

Self-supply contracts have accounted for the vast majority of renewable energy projects in Mexico, many of which are in the wind sector. Unless further policy changes make additional avenues more likely, these contracts will support future development as well. The "self-supply" model has even begun to expand outside the wind industry. Ford Motor Company agreed in June 2013, for example, to buy 3 MW from a 20 MW solar plant in Sonora.[72]

ITA anticipates further use of the "self-supply" model in the future and encourages exporters to identify Mexican companies that may be interested in developing a "self-supply" power plant, as developing projects this way seems like the fastest, more reliable method of doing business. The Foreign Commercial Service located in Mexico City can be a great supporter, helping interested American exporters develop a market entry strategy to this effect.

Opportunities for U.S. Companies

Wind
ITA expects wind energy to continue to be the dominant player in Mexico's renewable energy industry for the foreseeable future. Nearly 78 percent of the global investment in Mexico's renewable energy sector in 2012 supported wind energy development, most of which occurred in the Southern region of Oaxaca or in the state of Baja California. Several wind projects have been supplied by U.S.-made turbines and those turbines not made in the United States likely included several component parts made in the United States.

According to *Bloomberg New Energy Finance,* in addition to wind turbines, Mexico currently lacks the ability to manufacture bearings and gearboxes for the wind industry, indicating that any future wind energy development will require some imports.

Solar
Solar development remains woefully short of its potential in Mexico. With one of the world's most robust solar resources, ITA believes the market could support significant solar exports over the coming decade. Prices have fallen dramatically over the past two years, making solar energy competitive in many parts of Mexico, particularly for small and medium sized enterprises that already pay commercial tariffs for electricity that are among the highest in Latin America.

To date, developers have amassed initial permits to construct only 393.7 MW of new solar generation, mostly in northern regions, but additional development is likely as demand increases and prices continue to fall. It will be important for U.S. suppliers to stress to potential clients that buying decisions should be determined based on the long-term cost of solar technologies, positioning U.S. technology more effectively against lower-cost products made elsewhere.

Geothermal
Mexico has traditionally been one of the largest geothermal markets in the world, yet little development has occurred over the past decade. Many geothermal fields no longer produce as much power as they once did and new facilities have been difficult to develop.

However, recent indications from the Mexican Government, suggest new geothermal development could be on the way. The Energy Ministry recently began an effort to put increased focus on this renewable energy source by launching the "International Geothermal Energy Forum." Early-stage geothermal services should provide opportunities for U.S. exporters, including engineering services, resource exploration and drilling services, and well/resource confirmation.

Biomass
The Mexican biomass and waste-to-energy value chains are 100 percent complete, according to *Bloomberg New Energy Finance.*[73] As a result, though development will

continue, it is unlikely that the sector will support a significant amount of U.S. technology exports.

Hydropower
Development in the hydropower sector is likely to be focused on the small hydro industry, where U.S. exporters may find opportunities providing pipes, turbines, and engineering services to a relatively small and stagnant industry. Despite the lack of expected demand, Mexico still ranks 7th on ITA's list of top hydropower export markets based almost exclusively on the market share enjoyed by U.S. exporters

---

Upcoming Renewable Energy Trade Events for Exporters interested in Mexico:
- **Mexico Wind Power 2014**; *February 26-27, 2014* – Mexico City
- **Green Expo 2014**; *September 24-26, 2014* – Mexico City (for companies interested in Green Expo, contact Claudia Salgado at Claudia.Salgado@trade.gov)

U.S. Foreign Commercial Service Contact Information: Miguel Vazquez
Commercial Specialist
Email: miguel.vazquez@trade.gov
Tel: (5255)5140-2643

For more information, please visit: www.export.gov/reee or www.export.gov/mexico.

This page intentionally left blank

South Africa

Overall Rank: **12**

Type: Small Market; Small Market Share

The magnitude of South Africa's planned renewable energy expansion over the next decade is expected to support U.S. exports across several subsectors. South Africa is already the largest clean energy market in Africa; and the market can provide a base of operations for business development in other African markets. However, severe local content requirements and the presence of one, vertically-integrated electric utility can make exports difficult.

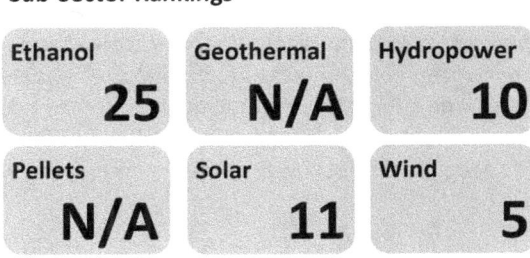

Sub-Sector Rankings

Ethanol	Geothermal	Hydropower
25	N/A	10

Pellets	Solar	Wind
N/A	11	5

South Africa is typically the first African market most American exporters consider when developing an export strategy. Its energy demand growth and economic vitality make it an attractive destination, as well as a base for future projects in other African markets.

For renewable energy companies, South Africa also offers tremendous resource potential across a wide array of technologies. Yet the market can be complex with relatively few buyers for U.S. products and services and strong local content requirements, as well as a predilection to buy lower cost equipment.

Overview of Renewable Energy Market

Renewable energy has only recently become an important topic in South Africa, as non-hydro renewables account for less than one percent of South Africa's current generating capacity. Today, the sector is dominated by a vertically integrated purchaser – the state-owned power company, Eskom – that is involved in all aspects of power generation, transmission, and distribution. In fact, Eskom generates roughly 95 percent of electricity consumed in South Africa, mostly from coal-fired power plants, and will continue to be the dominant player in the industry going forward.

While this can be good for U.S. exporters that provide products or services to Eskom, the market can be

difficult to enter for other firms without a strong prior relationship with the company. Fortunately, the South African Government has attempted to divide the power generation sector among Eskom and independent power producers (IPPs) to increase the participation of the private sector. ITA supports this effort, as it could create new buyers for American technology.

The South African Government expects the new IPPs will reduce costs for consumers through increased competition.[74] The South African Government also hopes the new IPPs will promote the development of new power plants, which are desperately needed. Several high profile electricity shortages have hit the country recently, threatening South Africa's continued economic growth and forcing policy makers to consider cleaner, more sustainable alternatives.

According to the South African Energy Department, the country will need over 40 GW of new generation capacity by 2025 to meet future demand. To help meet this objective, South Africa launched the Renewable Energy Independent Power Producer Program (REIPP) in August 2011, which established a bidding process for renewable energy projects and outlined the further expansion of renewable energy in the country. The REIPP's targets included 3,725 MW of renewable energy capacity to be installed by 2016. Of this, onshore wind was expected to contribute 1,850 MW, solar PV to contribute 1,450 MW, and concentrated solar power was expected to contribute an additional 200 MW.

In 2012, the South African Government increased its target, calling for an additional 3,200 MW to be added to the nation's electricity mix by 2020.[75] And in November 2011, it began the first of three tender announcements aimed at accelerating renewable energy development. In total, nearly 4 GW of new clean energy projects were tendered, with each receiving a 20-year power purchase agreement with ESKOM.[76]

As a result of the tenders, foreign investment – both from the private sector and international financial institutions – has grown considerably. The U.S. Government, through the Ex-Im Bank, and the Chinese Government, through the Industrial and Commercial Bank of China, each pledged to invest about $2 billion to fund clean energy projects.[77] And the Development Bank of Southern Africa approved a $1.1 billion loan for renewable energy projects in 2012.

Ex-Im's investment was bolstered by the creation of the U.S.-Africa Clean Energy Development Finance Center (CEDFC), an initiative developed by the Overseas Private Investment Corporation and the U.S. Trade and Development Agency. The CEDFC offers an important opportunity for U.S. exporters, providing the financial support many projects need and also helping to link American manufacturers to those projects.

Challenges and Barriers to Renewable Energy Exports

Renewable energy exporters to South Africa face several challenges. The most impactful is likely the country's intensifying local content requirements, which threaten to undermine the ability of several U.S. firms to do business in the country. Previously, U.S. exporters faced only a moderate LCR. While detrimental to export competiveness, the LCRs still allowed South African developers to purchase some products on international markets.

Most renewable energy projects were able to satisfy South Africa's 35 percent local content requirement through construction costs. In the most recent tender, however, local content requirements have increased to at least 40 percent (concentrated solar power projects are mandated to meet a 45 percent threshold). Developers, however, must reach a 65 percent local content threshold to maximize their bids' "social

economic score."[78] At this level of required local content, U.S. exports are severely threatened.

Another obstacle to U.S. renewable energy exports to South Africa is competition from foreign firms with support from their respective governments, particularly in the wind and solar sectors. Denmark, for instance, recently signed an agreement with South Africa pledging its financial support for wind power development, which is likely to help facilitate the use of Danish-made Vestas wind turbines.[79]

Chinese firms are particularly active in South Africa. Suntech, prior to its bankruptcy, was the first to enter the market, agreeing to supply PV equipment to two South African solar farms in July 2011. Jinko Solar and Yingli have also become active participants in the South African market and have offered bids in the country's public tenders.[80] Both companies have been supported heavily by the Chinese Government.

Opportunities for U.S. Companies

While ITA remains skeptical that South Africa will meet its renewable energy goals by 2025, the sector's growth should be strong enough through 2015 to support significant U.S. exports. South Africa does not currently have the manufacturing capacity to meet its strict localization requirements. In the short-term, U.S. firms should therefore seek out export opportunities, particularly by partnering with local companies.

Wind
Opportunities for U.S. exporters will be greatest in the wind energy sector. Areas that could provide the most potential for U.S. exports are financial consulting, construction, and balance-of-plant equipment. Given the high cost of transportation and competition from lower-cost manufacturers either domestically or from Asia, it is unlikely that American firms will export turbines, blades, or larger turbine components competitively.

Ethanol
South Africa's emerging biofuels market holds only limited opportunities for U.S. exporters. In October 2013, South Africa announced that biofuels must comprise at least 5 percent of diesel and 2-10 percent of gasoline by October 2015. At the same time, the country announced that *all* grain needed for this production must be produced locally. Thus, although U.S. firms could have provided feedstocks or fuel to the market prior to this policy change, only service

providers, consultants, or engineers are likely to benefit from the planned market expansion.

Solar

Interest in the solar sector in South Africa, in both PV and CSP technologies, is high, but much of the sector's growth is expected to occur post-2015. Though the U.S. market share in South Africa's solar market will be small, South Africa is one of the few solar markets globally that does not manufacture enough solar products to meet its own domestic demand. This should support a modest amount of U.S. exports, particularly if the projects are supported by Ex-Im financing.

Upcoming Renewable Energy Trade Events for Exporters interested in South Africa:
- **West Africa Energy Business Development Trade Mission**; *May 18 -23, 2014 –* Ghana and Nigeria
- **Webinar: Energy Opportunities in Sub-Saharan Africa**; *February 19; February 27; March 6* – all webinars at 10am Eastern.

U.S. Foreign Commercial Service Contact Information: Daniel S. Duane
Commercial Officer
Email: Daniel.Duane@trade.gov
Tel: (27 11) 290 3062

For more information, please visit: www.export.gov/reee or www.export.gov/southafrica.

This page intentionally left blank

United Kingdom

Overall Rank: **6**

Type: Large Market; Small Market Share

The United Kingdom (UK) is one of the few renewable energy markets that is projected to grow substantially, but will likely need to rely on significant imports of both technologies and feedstocks to meet expected demand. While export opportunities exist in most renewable energy sectors, U.S. wood pellet exports to the UK are expected to increase substantially and present the largest renewable energy export opportunity to the UK through 2015.

Sub-Sector Rankings

Ethanol	Geothermal	Hydropower
11	**N/A**	**N/A**

Pellets	Solar	Wind
1	**15**	**15**

Renewable energy in the United Kingdom is poised for significant growth over the next decade, with policy changes driving investment across a wide cross section of technologies. The UK Government has made clear its intentions to deploy renewable energy technologies at scale; and partnerships between the UK and overseas organizations have become increasingly viewed as an important means of fast-tracking the introduction of new products to the market. What is more, the UK is one of the few markets in the world where future growth will necessitate a substantial amount of imports to meet expected demand.

Although the UK's renewable energy market is large, the market share enjoyed by U.S. exporters is relatively small, particularly in renewable energy power generation. Future market growth is thus expected to only marginally benefit exporters looking to sell technology and expertise into the UK. For example, despite ranking in the top ten globally in both expected wind and solar capacity installations through 2015, neither subsector ranks highly in terms of export potential.

However, the UK has traditionally been a strong customer of renewable fuels from the United States. Although ethanol exports to the UK dropped dramatically in 2013 when the EU imposed antidumping duties, wood pellet exports more than doubled (from 673 million kg to over 1.7 billion kg) and significant

growth is projected to continue into the future, as the U.S. pellet industry is well positioned to continue being a top supplier to UK utilities.

Overview of the Renewable Energy Market

Under the European Renewable Energy Directive of 2009, the UK committed to deriving 15 percent of its energy consumption from renewable energy sources by 2020. Estimates indicate that in order to meet this goal, roughly 30 percent of the UK's electricity generation will need to come from renewable sources.[81] For the 2013/2014 period, the total renewable obligation level for utilities is 13.4 percent in Great Britain and 6.3 percent in Northern Ireland.[82]

For a decade, the UK has focused its policy support around a complicated certificate and quota scheme known as "the Renewables Obligation." Different technologies received differentiated levels of support through a "banding" mechanism that provides a certain number of Renewable Obligation Certificates (ROCs) per MWh of electricity produced. In April 2013, new ROC banding levels took effect, with offshore wind and marine technologies benefiting the most from new tariff levels, while onshore wind and solar ROCs decreased.[83]

Small projects, up to 5MW, are also eligible for feed-in tariffs. The FIT for small solar projects has been especially popular, with over 1.1GW of PV capacity installed in 2011 – 10 times the anticipated amount. Consequently, the government cut FIT rates to save money, prompting a legal dispute with the solar industry. It later attempted to bring more stability to the scheme by proposing predictable cuts, starting in 2012, to keep track of falling costs.

Several policies collectively known as "Comprehensive Electricity Market Reform" are expected to replace the Renewables Obligation as the primary support mechanism for the industry in the future. In particular, the reform effort is expected to attract the £110 billion investment that is needed to replace current generating capacity, upgrade the country's electricity grid by 2020, and cope with a rising demand for electricity.

Under the proposed reforms, the Renewables Obligation will close to new generators in March 2017. Electricity generation that is accredited under the Renewables Obligation will continue to receive its full lifetime of support (20 years) until the scheme closes in 2037. Beginning in 2027, the British Government will fix the price of the ROC for the remaining 10 years of the Renewables Obligation at its long-term value and buy the ROCs directly from renewable energy generators.[84] This is meant to reduce volatility in the final years of the scheme. The long-term value of a ROC will be the buyout price plus 10 percent.

Electricity market reform is also expected to include a carbon price floor, emissions performance standards, additional support for the Green Investment Bank that was launched in 2012, and "contracts for difference" which will ensure a certain level of profitability for renewable energy generation. On December 4, 2013, the UK Government's Department of Energy and Climate Change announced the final "strike price" that renewable energy developers will receive for projects brought online between 2014 and 2019 under the "contracts for difference scheme."

U.S. renewable energy exporters should continue to monitor the UK's policy environment closely, as any changes could facilitate new investment that may support export opportunities. In niche sectors like wood pellets that already enjoy a competitive position in the market, changes to policy – either positive or negative – may be impactful enough to dramatically change the attractiveness of the UK market relative to other potential export destinations.

Challenges and Barriers to Renewable Energy Exports

Despite projections for growth in the UK, several challenges limit U.S. exports into the future. First, competition from EU-based suppliers will continue to be strong. At a time of global oversupply of technology, the UK's status as one of the few markets that requires imports to meet its demand makes it one of the most attractive markets anywhere in the world. It also means that American exporters face competition from lower cost products manufactured elsewhere, as well as innovative products manufactured in Europe.

Additionally, many of the products demanded by the UK market are not produced in great quantity in the United States. In the wind sector, for example, the UK is increasingly focused on the development of offshore wind projects. Exporters in this sector should anticipate difficulty convincing potential buyers that their products or services can transition well from onshore projects in the United States to offshore projects in the UK.

Recent sustainability requirements for ethanol in the EU's Renewable Energy Directive, which took effect this year, are expected to slow the import of ethanol from the United States as well.[85] Moreover, the EU's recent decision to impose a five-year $83.03 per metric ton duty on U.S. ethanol imports that began in February 2013 will continue to diminish the attractiveness of ethanol produced in the United States.

Opportunities for U.S. Companies

Solar
In the solar sector, the UK enjoys only about 550 MW of module manufacturing capacity and very little cell manufacturing capacity. Yet, ITA expects the UK to install roughly 1.7 GW of solar capacity through 2015, mostly in the form of small-scale, roof-mounted installations. Most technologies will need to be imported, but because buyers will be individual consumers, it will be difficult for U.S. companies to capture market share without distributor agreements in place.

Wind
The wind energy sector is expected to make the largest contribution towards the UK Government's renewable target. The UK has more than 8.2 GW of installed wind capacity in operation. By 2015, estimates indicate that roughly 12.8 GW will be installed with most of the new capacity expected to come from offshore development. With relatively shallow waters and strong winds extending into the North Sea, the UK has the largest offshore wind resource in the world. The UK

Government has set aside £30million to support offshore wind development, with the goal of reaching 18 GW of offshore capacity by 2020.

Most U.S. wind exports to the UK will likely have to meet niche demands to be competitive, or be in the form of wind energy services. Financial expertise, environmental impact consultants, and engineers should all find some opportunities. Yet the competition for services in the UK wind market will be fierce, as the market is well developed and very mature.

Biomass

Biomass energy production (for both electricity and heat) offers another important opportunity for U.S. renewable energy exports. More than a third of the UK's renewable power comes from biomass. In fact, the UK has the highest industrial demand for wood pellets in the European Union and uses biomass in large power plants both as a stand-alone fuel or to co-fire with coal. In 2012, biomass capacity in the UK was 829 MW – a 400 percent over the last ten years.

The contribution of biomass to the UK's renewable energy mix is currently around 10 percent, but is forecasted to increase to nearly 25 percent by 2020. To meet this expected demand increase, power plant operators are expected to import 1 million tons of biomass wood pellets annually per 100MW capacity. The UK's domestic biomass supply is expected to fall drastically short of this amount, meeting only 5 to 10

percent of the projected demand by 2014. The low volume of UK supply means that every year power generators must import millions of tons of wood chips or pellets to meet their biomass needs.

British electrical power generation company Drax is likely to be the largest user of wood pellets in the world by the end of this decade. Drax is in the process of converting three of its six generating units at the coal-fired Drax Power Station (total capacity of approximately 4GW) in North Yorkshire to run on sustainable biomass. The actual timing of the conversion is dependent on biomass fuel sourcing. In 2012, Drax also decided to develop two U.S.-based pellet plants – in Mississippi and Louisiana, respectively – with a combined capacity of 900,000 tons a year, and to invest in a port facility in Louisiana with an annual export capacity of 3 million tons.

As a result, ITA expects significant commercial opportunities to emerge in the UK for U.S. biomass exporters. Already, most UK imports of wood pellets come from the United States and Canada; a trend which should continue through 2015. UK developers of biomass power plants are actively looking for credit worthy existing large industrial feedstock providers. U.S. suppliers interested in the UK market, however, must understand that they will need to deliver in a 2 years' timeframe (from the date in which a contract is signed) and that capacity of supply is paramount to finding success in the market.

Upcoming Renewable Energy Trade Events for Exporters interested in the United Kingdom:
- **EU Funds for Renewable Energy Cohesion (webinar)**; *January 2014*
- **Argus European Biomass Trading Conference**, *April 9-10, 2014* – London
- **"All-Energy" Renewable Energy Conference and Exhibition**; *May 21-22, 2014* – Aberdeen AEEC

U.S. Foreign Commercial Service Contact Information: Claudia Colombo
Commercial Specialist
Email: Claudia.Colombo@trade.gov
Tel: +44 (0) 20 7894 0443

For more information, please visit: www.export.gov/reee or www.export.gov/unitedkingdom.

This page intentionally left blank

Sector Snapshots

This section contains sector snapshots that summarize U.S. renewable energy export opportunities in each subsector. The overviews outline ITA's analysis of the export potential across each technology's supply chain and offer commentary on market dynamics that will impact the sector both in the near-term and into the future. The snapshots provide subsector rankings and describe the different types of markets U.S. exporters within each subsector must sell into. Finally, each snapshot offers commentary on the relative competitive position of U.S. suppliers.

This page intentionally left blank

Sector Case Study: Wind Energy

Most U.S. wind energy exports currently go to only a small group of markets – namely China, Canada, Mexico, and Brazil. These four markets alone are expected to account for over 75 percent of all U.S. wind exports through 2015. Yet, continued global investment in the wind industry outside traditional markets should increase in the near-term, likely broadening market opportunities. Exporters are encouraged to consider a range of factors when developing an export strategy, including expected demand, policy certainty, a market's distance from production, and the availability of lower cost technologies.

The wind industry is a large and growing sector with a supply chain that produces thousands of component parts and a service sector that is increasingly advanced in its use of technology to design turbines, organize wind farms, and map wind potential. Most of the industry is vertically integrated, but deep supply chains have emerged to provide technology and components to the largest turbine manufacturers.

Though the wind market is becoming increasingly global, most U.S. exports go to a small number of countries. The top four export destinations – China, Canada, Mexico, and Brazil – account for over 75 percent of all U.S. wind exports. At the same time, these markets account for less than half the total value of the global import market.

Overview of Global Export Market Opportunities

By 2015, ITA expects nearly 65 GW of new wind capacity to be brought online outside the United States, a nearly 25 percent increase over the size of the current non-U.S. market. Most of this demand will be met with locally-sourced products, as the wind industry's preferred method of global expansion has increasingly been foreign direct investment.

The current share of the global wind import market captured by U.S. exporters is small – reaching only 2-3 percent. Fortunately, ITA expects the global market to shift away from traditional European markets through 2015 and towards a more global industry where U.S. exports may be more competitive.

Today, seven of the world's largest wind markets are in Europe. Yet over the next two years, six of the ten largest markets will be non-European countries, including China, India, Brazil, Canada, Turkey, and Australia. China, in particular, will be the focal point of the industry, installing roughly 25 GW of new capacity, nearly five times as much as India – the second largest expected market outside the United States through 2015.

Top Wind Export Markets through 2015

1. **China**
   (small share; large market)

2. **Canada**
   (large share; small market)

3. **Mexico**
   (large share; small market)

4. **Brazil**
   (large share; large market)

5. **South Africa**
   (large share; small market)

6. **Korea**
   (small share; large market)

7. **Uruguay**
   (large share; small market)

8. **Guatemala**
   (large share; small market)

9. **Vietnam**
   (large share; small market)

10. **Costa Rica**
    (large share; small market)

An export strategy focused on these markets may increase the likelihood of success for many exporters, although each market is different and exporters are encouraged to understand the nuances of each potential opportunity. In China, U.S. exporters capture only a tiny percentage of an overall market that is immense and growing quickly. In Brazil, U.S. exporters would capture an even larger share of the market, but are hampered by significant local content provisions and high import tariffs. And in Canada and Mexico, exporters often find success based on the close integration of supply chains in these countries, not because the markets are particularly large.

Canada and Mexico are in fact indicative of the types of markets where U.S. wind exporters are often the most competitive. Six of the top ten markets for U.S. wind exports are located in the Western Hemisphere; a fact that is directly reflective of the market share captured by U.S. exporters in these countries.

The Wind Energy Export Opportunity in the Near-Term

Wind energy exports in the near-term are expected to be highly differentiated depending on the type of technology or service offered. For service providers, developers of small component parts, or high-tech control equipment, markets in Asia that are growing quickly and increasingly seeking high-tech solutions may offer greater opportunities. In China, for example, where re-powering existing wind farms with new technology has become a priority, American companies that can provide technology solutions may find considerable demand for their expertise. Exporters, however, should be highly mindful of threats to their intellectual property, which can be significant.

For manufacturers of large component parts, Latin American markets may provide the greatest opportunity – particularly when pairing their technology with Ex-Im financing. While these markets will not be the largest wind markets globally, they may provide an attractive cost environment in which to do business.

In Latin America, two important competitors have emerged that companies should consider when developing an export strategy for the region. Chinese manufacturers now compete directly with American exporters in many Latin American markets – a new phenomenon, since Chinese manufacturers traditionally focused exclusively on China's domestic market. One example is a recent wind deal announced in Chile that will use Goldwind turbines. In the past, the project would likely have been sourced from the United States, but low-cost Chinese turbines and cheap financing offered by the Chinese export-import bank was enough for Goldwind to win the bid.

The second key competitor is Brazil, which has used *de facto* local content requirements through its national development bank and high import tariffs to protect and grow its domestic manufacturing base. Brazil now has the capability of supplying wind technologies to markets elsewhere in South America. This capability has been limited to date, but stands to increase as the Brazilian wind market continues to expand.

Planning for the Long-Term

Bloomberg New Energy Finance predicts that the annual wind market will reach 78 GW globally by 2020 and cumulative installations will total 1,600 GW by 2030,[86] resulting in a $2.7 trillion investment opportunity.[87] While some of the industry's growth will occur in the United States.

As exporters begin planning for the long-term, ITA encourages efforts to be focused on developing market-specific strategies, or the development of niche products or services that are unlikely to be commoditized. Some markets, particularly in Europe, will likely become increasingly focused on offshore projects, while in others, increasing the efficiency and output of existing projects will become a market driver.

The U.S. Government remains committed to supporting wind energy exporters wherever in the world opportunities arise. Given the large transportation costs associated with shipping several wind products, U.S. exporters may want to consider utilizing Ex-Im financing, which can provide buyers of technology the cost-competitive financing needed to make deals attractive. In addition, ITA staff located at U.S. Export Assistance Centers around the country are ready to assist in the planning, development, and implementation of export market plans for any wind energy exporter.

Sector Case Study: Solar Energy

The U.S. solar industry is expected to face a changing and increasingly challenging global environment in which to sell its products and services through 2015. In the short-term, exporters are likely to encounter several trade barriers that limit the competitiveness of U.S.-made products, as well as the continued over-supply of technology – though prices should continue to stabilize in many markets. As new emerging markets develop, exporters should be well-positioned to take advantage of opportunities in non-European countries, particularly in Latin America.

Since 2008, the solar industry has grown rapidly as a source of energy and economic activity, both in the United States and around the world. The industry involves a wide range of companies, each with different needs, opportunities, and challenges.

Today, the solar industry is decidedly global. Manufacturers are often headquartered in one country but operate worldwide, shipping products easily across borders. Large companies often have supply chains in several countries at once, importing components from many different suppliers.

Overview of Global Export Market Opportunities

For many American manufacturers of solar technologies, the dramatic price declines of the past few years have caused significant hardship. Yet, for installers and developers of solar projects the drop in prices has led to higher profits and an exponential increase in the deployment of solar products. In fact, nearly three-quarters of all solar capacity in the United States has been deployed in the last two years – largely mirroring the drop in solar prices.

Globally, the trend of accelerated deployment is expected to continue relatively unabated. Over the next two years, ITA conservatively estimates that 47 GW of new solar capacity will be installed outside the United States – more than 50 percent of total worldwide capacity currently online. This estimate is substantially more conservative than some industry sources, which suggest as much as 73 GW of installed during the same period.

The market is undergoing a significant transition away from Europe – the historical driver of the industry's demand – towards a truly global industry. In 2011, 70

percent of the world's PV modules were installed in Europe;[88] and Europe accounted for seven of the world's ten largest solar markets. Today, most of the industry's growth is occurring outside of Europe, led predominantly by China and Japan.

Importantly, the world's largest solar markets have traditionally not been the largest export markets for U.S. companies. Since 2007, out of the ten largest markets for U.S. solar exports, only two were in the top

Top Solar Export Markets through 2015

1. **Canada**
   (large share; large market)

2. **Chile**
   (large share; large market)

3. **Israel**
   (large share; small market)

4. **China**
   (small share; large market)

5. **France**
   (small share; large market)

6. **India**
   (large share; large market)

7. **Denmark**
   (large share; small market)

8. **Japan**
   (small share; large market)

9. **Belgium**
   (small share; small market)

10. **Italy**
    (small share; small market)

---

ten markets globally in terms of solar installations: Germany and Spain. ITA expects this trend to continue through 2015 and predicts that China and Japan will account for roughly 10 percent of U.S. solar exports, but over half the installed capacity brought online outside the United States.

U.S. exporters have generally been hampered by the existence of strong local competitors in European markets and the cost advantage enjoyed by many exporters from Asia. China, for example, accounts for over half the global manufacturing capacity in the solar industry and, until recently, exported almost all of the products it produces.

The cost disadvantage has been intensified by the presence of local content requirements in several key markets, including India, Canada, South Africa, and Saudi Arabia. These requirements, as well high import duties in other markets, have been used to protect local industries in many markets that view solar development as key to the establishment of high-tech domestic manufacturing bases. Despite several trade cases within the World Trade Organization, it is likely that in the near-term similar burdensome policy regimes will continue to plague the industry's export potential. U.S. firms are highly encouraged to report trade restrictive practices to U.S. embassy or consulate officials or to contact their local U.S. Export Assistance Center.

Additionally, in some Asian markets, burdensome technology certification regimes have also been used to keep U.S. products out of the market. Korea and Japan are routinely identified by U.S. exporters as markets where technology certification is used deliberately to provide advantages for domestic companies.

The Solar Energy Export Opportunity in the Near-Term

The current overcapacity situation is not expected to abate before 2015 and will continue to define the export opportunity for U.S. firms in the short-term. Although the situation has eased slightly over the past year, with capacity ratios for top tier manufacturers exceeding 80 percent in 2013 and expected to increase further through 2014 and beyond.[89] Thus while downward trending prices should continue, prices are expected to stabilize, allowing U.S. solar exporters to enter more confidently into international markets.

ITA expects that the largest export markets for U.S. companies through 2015 will be markets that lack sufficient manufacturing capacity to meet expected

demand. For example, Canada and Chile – the top two projected export destinations – are expected to install several new solar projects, but will need to import equipment to complete these projects. As in other markets with a need to import technology, competition will be fierce (particularly with an oversupply of technology globally), but given the large market share enjoyed by U.S. exporters in these markets, U.S. companies should find considerable opportunities.

In fact, ITA expects Canada and Chile to account for over half of all exports in the sector through 2015 – a proportion that would increase if more development takes place in these markets than what is projected. Beyond Canada and Chile, the export market should remain relatively confined. The top 10 export markets are expected to account for 90 percent of all exports in the sector. To win in these markets, it will be important for exporters to differentiate the quality and reliability of their products from those offered by lower cost suppliers, as this is often the reason buyers decide to purchase U.S. technology.

Planning for the Long-Term

Although short-term competitiveness challenges and the occasional negative headline can invoke pessimism, it is important for solar exporters to understand the industry's vast long-term potential. The International Energy Agency predicts that the deployment of solar technologies will expand rapidly over the next two decades, helping renewables approach coal as the world's leading source of energy by 2035.

Many of the world's largest solar markets beyond 2015 will be in places that have little or no solar market development to date. India and Saudi Arabia, for example, have put targets in place that – if met – would position them as leading solar markets for decades to come. The race to deploy solar technologies is therefore shifting markedly towards Asia. Unfortunately, these markets are not places where U.S. exporters currently enjoy a significant market share, presenting export challenges for U.S. companies.

To compete in these new markets, U.S. exporters will likely need to further their technological lead through continued innovation. Buyers around the world often look to the United States for the latest technology and maintaining this comparative advantage over lower-cost suppliers will likely be critical to long-term competitiveness.

Sector Case Study: Geothermal Energy

The United States is the world's leading geothermal market with a supply chain of manufacturers and service providers ready and able to export their products and expertise around the world. Unfortunately, growth in the geothermal sector globally remains limited compared to other renewable energy subsectors, with most export opportunities tied to post-2015 projects. In the near-term, ITA expects ineffective policy regimes and poor market conditions to allow only a handful of projects to move through development and ultimately to commission. Exporters are encouraged to position themselves now for opportunities in the future by introducing their technology or services to local procurement officials or development firms.

No country produces as much geothermal energy as the United States. Installed capacity reached 3.4 GW domestically in 2012, nearly thirty percent of all geothermal capacity installed globally.

Yet geothermal export opportunities have traditionally been limited by the lack of development occurring in foreign markets. Nevertheless, at the end of 2013, the Geothermal Energy Association had identified 70 countries that were advancing nearly 700 new geothermal projects. In 2007, a similar report found that only 46 countries were actively developing geothermal projects.[90] As new technologies are brought to market that provide opportunities to produce geothermal energy in locations previously unavailable to the industry, growth should continue into the future.

Overview of Global Export Market Opportunities

The geothermal industry is reliant on the availability of naturally occurring geothermal reservoirs and, as such, has thus far been limited to markets near tectonic fault lines. The top five markets in terms of installed geothermal capacity – the United States, the Philippines, Indonesia, Mexico, and New Zealand – all exist along the so-called "ring of fire." These countries collectively account for over two-thirds of the world's total installed geothermal capacity, which reached 11.4 GW in 2013.

Bloomberg New Energy Finance projects that total installed capacity globally will increase only 1.5 GW over the next two years.[91] However, near term capacity additions do not generally reflect export opportunities, because of the long project cycle for geothermal power

plants. Procurement decisions are typically made about three years in advance of the project's expected completion date. Fortunately, the global pipeline of announced projects includes 13.2 GW – a pipeline that exceeds the entirety of global capacity currently online. The increased capacity is expected to come from more than 300 different projects that should come online in

Top Geothermal Export Markets to 2015

1. **Kenya**
   (large share; large market)

2. **New Zealand**
   (small share; large market)

3. **Turkey**
   (large share; large market)

4. **Indonesia**
   (small share; large market)

5. **Japan**
   (small share; large market)

6. **Philippines**
   (small share; large market)

7. **Chile**
   (large share; small market)

8. **Ethiopia**
   (small share; small market)

9. **El Salvador**
   (large share; small market)

10. **Iceland**
    (small share; large market)

the medium-term, creating important export opportunities for American firms in the near-term.

Most of this development will occur around 2020 when policy and regulatory frameworks being developed now begin to materialize into completed geothermal power plants. Indonesia is expected to account for the most geothermal capacity growth with 3.2 GW of capacity currently under development. The Philippines, Kenya, and Chile are expected to account for a further 2.5 GW of development[92] – although Chile has yet to bring any capacity online so future development is relatively uncertain.

Importantly, unlike other sectors where project development is both quicker and more consistent, many announced geothermal projects never reach completion. Instead, projects are often neglected out of resource concerns, a lack of policy support, or development opportunities that occur elsewhere. *Bloomberg New Energy Finance* notes that less than half of the capacity planned to be brought online between 2015 and 2017 will likely never be fully commissioned.[93]

The Geothermal Energy Export Opportunity in the Near-Term

The United States enjoys a strong competitive position within the global geothermal market. U.S. companies enjoy significant market share both in terms of development and component part shipments. Unfortunately, global investment in geothermal projects is expected to be less than one percent of total renewable energy investment through 2015.

According to ITA's analysis, Kenya, New Zealand, Turkey, Indonesia, Japan, the Philippines, Chile, and Ethiopia will account for over 90 percent of all geothermal exports through 2015. Kenya alone will likely account for over half of all geothermal exports – a fact supported by anecdotal evidence and the growing list of planned geothermal projects in the country. Unlike other markets where geothermal projects can be difficult to finance, projects in Kenya appear to enjoy an easier time attracting investors and thus move quicker through the development cycle.

U.S. exporters may also find short-term export opportunities exporting geothermal heat pump technologies. While not considered directly in the *Top Markets* analysis, demand for geothermal heat pumps appears to be increasing globally with U.S. companies enjoying significant market share.

Planning for the Long-Term

Over the next two decades growth in the global geothermal market should accelerate, as power demands continue to increase worldwide and the cost of geothermal production becomes more attractive. *Bloomberg New Energy Finance* expects online geothermal capacity to double over the next 17 years with 610 to 950 MW of new capacity added worldwide every year.[94]

ITA expects the trend of most new projects utilizing "flash" technologies will continue. Most projects currently under development are greenfield projects at a site that is yet to confirm the expected resource via full diameter deep drilling (the industry standard), but drilling has commenced at those sites that are expected to be "high-grade flash" resources.

This may ultimately limit component exports, as Japanese firms continue to dominate this market segment. However, ITA expects considerable export opportunities to develop for U.S. geothermal service companies – something in which the United States already excels.

As investment continues to flow into the natural gas drilling market, the skills and companies that develop should be well positioned to provide geothermal services to projects overseas – as the skill set for both industries is similar. Deploying geothermal drilling rigs in foreign markets, however, is decidedly difficult. For example, according to industry reports, a rig from the United States arriving in Chile must enter the country dismantled, packed in 70 different shipping containers.[95] Such practices add costs and limit the likelihood that developers will utilize U.S.-based service providers if there is a local rig ready to assist in a drilling effort.

Most geothermal drilling contracts lease the equipment that is used in the resource assessment. OPIC's announcement in the Renewable Energy and Energy Efficiency Export Initiative that it would support the leasing of U.S. renewable energy equipment is therefore of critical importance to the long-term export potential of the geothermal industry. For more information on OPIC's financing options, visit http://www.opic.gov/what-we-offer/financial-products.

Sector Case Study: Hydropower

The global hydropower industry is large and dynamic, as growth continues almost unabated in both large and small hydro capacity. The involvement of U.S.-based technology suppliers in the sector, however, remains severely limited, as the market is dominated by five foreign turbine manufacturers and continues to demand technologies and services for the large hydropower industry. U.S. hydropower exporters enjoy a more competitive position in the hydropower service market and within the "small hydro" market, particularly when projects are constructed closer to the United States.

On a global scale, hydropower capacity exceeds all other renewable energy sources combined. In fact, despite little attention, nearly 20 percent of global investment in renewable energy through 2015 is expected to be in the hydropower industry. Total installed hydropower capacity worldwide likely reached 800 GW in 2013 with new installations occurring mostly in developing country markets. The United States (79 GW) has the third largest installed hydropower capacity globally behind only China (229 GW) and Brazil (84 GW).[96]

Overview of Global Export Market Opportunities

The vast majority of the hydropower sector's growth is occurring outside the United States, and has been for some time. The industry installed roughly 26 GW of new capacity in 2012 – led by China (14 GW) – and is expected to continue to grow into the future. China alone enjoys a project pipeline of 80 GW including 16 different large hydropower projects.[97] In total, *Bloomberg New Energy Finance* notes a global project pipeline of 197 GW.[98]

China's growth, along with the rest of the world's, is mainly a reflection of interest in constructing large hydropower facilities. Large hydro receives the lion's share of global investment in the sector, accounting for roughly 85 percent of total new capacity brought online last year.[99] In fact, there are currently 44 mega-hydropower plants under development, each with more than 1 GW of planned capacity.

Through 2015, ITA expects 67 GW of new capacity to be brought online including both new builds and upgrades to existing facilities. China alone should

account for 22 GW of this new capacity, followed distantly by Ethiopia, Russia, Brazil, and Canada.

Regardless of location, almost all new large hydropower projects will be supplied with turbines from one of five dominant turbine producers.[100] European producers Andritz (Austrian), Alstom (French), and Voith (German) are likely to continue to dominate turbine sales outside

Top Hydropower Export Markets to 2015

1. **Canada**
   (large share; large market)

2. **Chile**
   (large share; small market)

3. **Russia**
   (small share; large market)

4. **Venezuela**
   (large share; small market)

5. **Colombia**
   (large share; small market)

6. **India**
   (small share; large market)

7. **Mexico**
   (large share; small market)

8. **Australia**
   (small share; large market)

9. **El Salvador**
   (small share; small market)

10. **South Africa**
    (small share; small market)

This *Top Markets* case study is provided as a resource for U.S. exporters by the International Trade Administration. Every effort has been made to ensure that the information presented in this report is complete and accurate as of the date of publication; however, the U.S. Government assumes no responsibility or liability for any errors or omissions. Readers are advised to independently verify any information contained in this intelligence brief prior to relying on it. The information provided in this report does not constitute legal advice. Readers are further advised to conduct their own due diligence and seek the advice of legal counsel before entering into business ventures or other commercial arrangements in this market.

of China, while Dongfang Electric and Harbin Electric will capture almost all turbine contracts in China. Component part manufacturers for large hydropower projects looking to export abroad will likely need to develop supplier relationships with one of these firms to be successful.

The Hydropower Export Opportunity in the Near-Term

While the United States does not enjoy a particularly competitive position within the large hydropower market, the three dominant European turbine manufactures all have some capacity in the United States and often export from their U.S. facilities for projects in Canada and Latin America. This explains why Canada ranks so highly on ITA's list of top export markets for the sector.

ITA believes hydropower will account for 15 percent of renewable energy exports through 2015. Canada alone will account for 78 percent of all exports in the sector despite installing just seven percent of new capacity worldwide. By contrast, China – by far the largest hydropower market over the next two years – will account for less than one percent of U.S. hydropower exports; a strong indication of the lack of competitiveness U.S. exporters enjoy in China.

Many of the hydropower projects constructed in Canada actually support cross-border electricity trade to the United States. According to the Canadian Hydro Association, approximately 80 percent of cross-border electricity exports from Canada are in the form of hydropower.[101]

The United States holds a strong position in the small hydro industry – generally defined as projects below 30 MW. The industry provides power to off-grid communities, small towns along rivers, and can generate power from existing dams used for other purposes. Since most new hydropower projects in the United States fall into this category, U.S. companies have developed an expertise that can be exported competitively to other markets.

Demand for small hydropower solutions may increase in markets facing either a loss of power capacity from existing large hydro facilities (perhaps as a result of droughts) or an electorate increasingly frustrated with the environmental degradation often associated with large hydropower development. The sustainability and reliability of new U.S. technologies will likely be the factors to encourage potential overseas deals.

In addition, a substantial share of the hydropower market is dedicated to the replacement of existing capacity, which often requires engineering and technical expertise. Several U.S. firms excel in this part of the hydropower supply chain and should benefit from capacity upgrades globally.

Planning for the Long-Term

Most large hydropower projects install turbines over several years, indicating that the project pipeline under development today will not be completed by 2015. However, in the medium-term, the hydropower market should begin to broaden by including newer and often smaller hydropower technologies that should allow U.S. exporters to compete more effectively. Wave and tidal energy developers, component part suppliers, and turbine manufacturers, for example, stand to make significant strides towards full commercialization within the next decade, opening new opportunities

As small run-of-river technologies that can produce power for rural, off-grid projects continue to be developed and commercialized, U.S. exporters will likely experience a technology advantage over firms from other markets. ITA encourages firms developing these technologies to devise export plans and market entry strategies now to take advantage of the opportunities created by this favorable export scenario. This may entail participation in trade missions, attendance at trade shows, and other activities to introduce concepts and new products to markets that may be unfamiliar with advances in technology development.

Sector Case Study: Biomass Pellets

Substitution of coal mixed with biomass in several European Union (EU) Member States to meet carbon emission targets is driving demand for biomass pellets produced in the United States. This has also spurred European investment in several new pellet mills in the American Southeast. In addition, exporters may find new opportunities in Asian markets, though these remain largely untapped by U.S. exporters. Exporters are encouraged to work closely with ITA and the U.S. Department of Agriculture's Foreign Agricultural Service to identify export opportunities.

Biomass power uses organic matter (wood, agricultural waste, etc) or inorganic matter like municipal solid waste to create electricity or heat. Wood pellets and wood chips are the most commonly used fuel in biomass power plants. Pellets are often the byproduct of the timber industry and can be created using residues from other processes.

U.S. wood pellet manufacturers can now produce over 16 billion metric tons of pellets annually.[102] Much of this production has been added in recent years for export to Europe. Trade in wood pellets for bioenergy has become so robust that in 2012 the World Customs Organization adopted a six-digit Harmonized Schedule code (440131) for wood pellets, making it easier to track global trade.[103] In 2012, nearly 1.9 million metric tons were exported, and in 2013 that number increased to 2.9 million metric tons.

Demand is so high that in the past two years, the Southeast United States, which has vast biomass resources, has witnessed a boom in pellet mill development. Some of these mills are even owned and operated by European electric utilities in an effort to secure their supply of pellets into the future, principally to meet EU-mandated emissions targets.

Overview of Global Export Market Opportunities

Over the next two years, ITA expects biomass pellet consumption in 21 key export markets to total 93.5 billion kilograms. China, which is ramping up its use of biomass power, will account for over one-fourth of this, but will take in only a small amount of exports. The United Kingdom will represent the next largest pellet market globally and is expected to support the most U.S. exports in the short-term.

The Pellet Export Opportunity in the Near-Term

The results showing mostly European countries as top markets for U.S. wood pellets are in line with expectations. According to the U.S. Industrial Pellet Association, in 2012 the United States was the leading exporter of wood pellets to the EU, capturing 36 percent of the EU's import market.[104] The top EU markets for U.S. pellet exporters were the UK (30 percent of EU imports), the Netherlands (24 percent),

Top Pellet Export Markets to 2015

1. **United Kingdom**
   (large share; large market)

2. **The Netherlands**
   (large share; large market)

3. **Belgium**
   (large share; large market)

4. **Turkey**
   (large share; small market)

5. **Korea**
   (small share; large market)

6. **Italy**
   (small share; large market)

7. **Denmark**
   (small share; large market)

8. **Sweden**
   (small share; large market)

9. **Canada**
   (small share; small market)

10. **Mexico**
    (small share; small market)

and Belgium (16 percent).[105] EU imports have steadily increased in the last five years, with imports of 2.5 million MT in 2008 and 4.5 million MT in 2012.[106] The increase is expected to continue, with projections ranging between 25 and 70 million MT by 2020.[107]

In the UK, the use of wood pellets in power plants is driven by the interaction of three policies:

- The Renewables Obligation Certificate (ROC), which requires until 2027 that licensed UK electricity suppliers source a specified proportion of the electricity they provide to customers from eligible renewable sources;

- The EU's Industrial Emissions Directive, which created a legally binding standard for sulfur dioxide emissions and is set to be implemented on January 1,2016; and

- The Carbon Price Floor, which disincentivizes the use of coal in coal-fired power plants.

On August 22, 2013, the UK's Department of Energy and Climate Change announced the release of its final guidelines, which stakeholders within the United States viewed as achievable based on current practices. The UK announced that the guidelines' sustainability criteria will be enforced starting in April 2015 and that it would not revise them until 2027 at the earliest.

In Asia, South Korea is likely the largest export opportunity for American exporters in the near term. In 2012, U.S. wood pellet producers exported less than 200,000 kilograms (kg) to Korea, but in 2013, exports to Korea exceeded 34 million kg. According to the government's targets, Korea's wood pellet demand is projected to grow from 750,000 MT in 2012 to 5 million MT by 2020. It also relies heavily on imports for forest products in general, with a forest products self-sufficiency rate of only 6 percent.[108] By comparison, a majority of the wood pellets used in China are expected to be manufactured in China, limiting export opportunities.

Shipments of U.S. wood pellets to the United States' NAFTA partners are surprisingly low. Canadian use of wood pellets has yet to catch up with production. The United States would be well positioned to supply pellets to Mexico, but new biomass electricity capacity is not expected to come online in the near term.

Planning for the Long-Term

Beyond 2015, demand for wood pellets should continue to grow, particularly in markets where emissions policies encourage the use of co-firing or dedicated biomass. This includes markets outside Europe. In Korea, for example, a policy mandate from the Government has increased demand for pellets from the U.S., dramatically increasing exports over the past two years. Similar policy incentives from other Asian markets may have similar impacts – particularly for pellet manufactures in the American Northwest, which would be well positioned geographically to supply product to growing Asian markets.

Sector Case Study: Ethanol

As more countries mandate the blending of ethanol, new export opportunities for U.S. ethanol producers are emerging. While exports to Europe are expected to decrease over the short term due to antidumping duties, countries in Latin America remain reliable trading partners. In addition, ethanol exports to Asian countries like the Philippines and Korea are likely to increase as well. Through 2015, however, Canada and Brazil should remain the two largest export destinations for U.S. ethanol, as most exports will likely be destined for one of these two markets.

The United States is the world's largest single producer and consumer of ethanol, followed by Brazil. Ethanol is a biofuel that is produced from a variety of sources (feedstocks), such as corn, wheat, sugar cane, sugar beet, and molasses. Less common feedstocks for ethanol include wood, municipal solid waste, and cellulosic materials from agricultural waste.

Ethanol trade is growing across the globe, as countries either mandate or incentivize blending with gasoline. These policies are often motivated partly by the need to reduce greenhouse gas emissions or air pollution, and partly by the desire to be less dependent on oil imports.

Overview of Global Export Market Opportunities

The overall volume of ethanol exports decreased over the 2011-2012 timeframe due to an extreme drought. However, in 2013, corn production had a complete rebound and there is expected to be a significant supply of ethanol in the immediate future. Nevertheless, due to the fragmented and diverse ethanol resources produced globally, U.S. exports in 2014-2015 will likely only capture 6 percent of non-U.S. global consumption Over the next two years, exports of U.S. ethanol to Europe are expected to be limited. Formerly one-third of all U.S. ethanol exports, by the end of 2013 only seven percent of exports were shipped to Europe (and an even smaller percentage to the EU member states). This decline is attributed by U.S. industry to the imposition in February 2013 of antidumping duties, which are being challenged in the EU courts.

Nevertheless, total exports of ethanol in 2013 were valued at over $1.5 billion. Over half of U.S. ethanol exports in 2013 were shipped to Canada, and industry is developing other markets such as Mexico, Peru, and the Philippines.

The Ethanol Export Opportunity in the Near-Term

Through 2015, Canada and Brazil are expected to import more ethanol than any other market. Both markets have historically been key export destination for ethanol producers in the United States, and several firms enjoy considerable commercial relationships with producers, suppliers, and other parts of the ethanol supply chain in these locations.

Top Ethanol Export Markets to 2015

1. **Canada**
   (large share; large market)

2. **Brazil**
   (large share; large market)

3. **Nigeria**
   (large share; large market)

4. **Peru**
   (large share; large market)

5. **Mexico**
   (large share; small market)

6. **Philippines**
   (large share; large market)

7. **Jamaica**
   (large share; small market)

8. **Netherlands**
   (small share; large market)

9. **Finland**
   (large share; small market)

10. **Korea**
    (small share; large market)

ITA, however, also strongly encourages U.S. exporters to position themselves for opportunities that are emerging in Asia. In particular, India is beginning to enforce its blending requirements and thus far does not have sufficient domestic ethanol supply to meet its expected demand. The end of 2013 saw significant shipments to China for the first time, despite a *de facto* bias towards the domestic industry. Exporters will likely experience strong competition in Asia from suppliers in Thailand, where the Thai Government is aggressively pursuing policies to increase ethanol production. In 2012, Thai producers exported over 300 million liters of ethanol, mostly to other Asian destinations like the Philippines, Singapore, and Korea.

Consumption of ethanol in the EU is expected to continue to rise in the near term, but exports from the United States remain stymied by antidumping duties in Europe. In addition, some U.S. ethanol exporters will face sustainability certification requirements under the Renewable Energy Directive that may limit their access to the market, as all biofuels producers importing product into the EU must provide evidence that they have reduced greenhouse gas emissions by at least 35 percent compared to fossil fuels. The mandate increases after 2017, requiring a verified reduction of at least 50 percent, and at least 60 percent for new installations.

On top of this, several EU member states have developed national voluntary systems, in addition to the 13 voluntary schemes adopted by the European Commission.[109] And even more regulation could be on the way, as the EU continues to debate limits on crop-based ethanol as part of the EU's overall 10 percent mandate, causing uncertainty even for European producers. As a result, ITA anticipates significant difficulty for U.S. ethanol exporters in the EU and possibly a further reduction in market share through 2015.

Planning for the Long-Term

Demand for ethanol is expected to increase into the medium-and-long-term. Several countries have intensifying mandates for ethanol use, particularly to limit the carbon emissions associated with vehicle fleets. As the world's leading producer of ethanol, this expected growth should provide considerable export opportunities. Companies are encouraged to work closely with ITA and the Foreign Agricultural Service of the U.S. Department of Agriculture to ensure they are ready and able to take advantage of export opportunities when they arise.

However, U.S. exporters should remain mindful of several barriers to continued long-term growth, including antidumping duties, sustainability certification requirements, and protectionist policies that require buyers to purchase ethanol from local producers. In some markets, such South Africa, blending is limited to domestically produced ethanol.

Appendix 1: Full Country Rankings

Below please find the complete rankings of all 75 markets considered in the analysis. Rankings are broken into overall rankings and subsector rankings.

Overall Renewable Energy Market Rankings

1	Canada	36	Sweden	71	Pakistan
2	China	37	Kuwait	72	Paraguay
3	Brazil	38	New Zealand	73	Lebanon
4	Chile	39	Qatar	74	Ecuador
5	Mexico	40	El Salvador	75	Sri Lanka
6	United Kingdom	41	Indonesia		
7	Nigeria	42	Egypt		
8	Peru	43	Ukraine		
9	Belgium	44	Taiwan		
10	Philippines	45	Spain		
11	Netherlands	46	Ireland		
12	South Africa	47	United Arab Emirates		
13	Kenya	48	Ethiopia		
14	Israel	49	Portugal		
15	India	50	Malaysia		
16	Korea	51	Lithuania		
17	Japan	52	Saudi Arabia		
18	Denmark	53	Iceland		
19	France	54	Morocco		
20	Colombia	55	Norway		
21	Jamaica	56	Hong Kong		
22	Venezuela	57	Nicaragua		
23	Russia	58	Ghana		
24	Guatemala	59	Greece		
25	Italy	60	Hungary		
26	Uruguay	61	Panama		
27	Costa Rica	62	Austria		
28	Vietnam	63	Romania		
29	Turkey	64	Estonia		
30	Germany	65	Slovakia		
31	Honduras	66	Bulgaria		
32	Finland	67	Czech Republic		
33	Thailand	68	Poland		
34	Australia	69	Algeria		
35	Argentina	70	Tunisia		

Wind Energy Market Rankings

1	China	41	Romania
2	Canada	42	France
3	Mexico	43	Indonesia
4	Brazil	44	Turkey
5	South Africa	45	New Zealand
6	Korea	46	Norway
7	Uruguay	47	Poland
8	Guatemala	48	Czech Republic
9	Vietnam	49	Sweden
10	Costa Rica	50	Taiwan
11	Philippines	51	Austria
12	Honduras	52	Slovakia
13	Colombia	53	Greece
14	Chile	54	Bulgaria
15	United Kingdom		
16	Kenya		
17	Belgium		
18	India		
19	Egypt		
20	Israel		
21	Thailand		
22	Germany		
23	Venezuela		
24	Lithuania		
25	Netherlands		
26	Italy		
27	Argentina		
28	Peru		
29	Russia		
30	Japan		
31	Portugal		
32	Hong Kong		
33	Finland		
34	Morocco		
35	Spain		
36	Hungary		
37	Australia		
38	Ukraine		
39	Ireland		
40	Estonia		

To Solar Export Markets			
1	Canada	41	Algeria
2	Chile	42	Tunisia
3	Israel	43	Czech Republic
4	China	44	Netherlands
5	France	45	Morocco
6	India	46	Sweden
7	Denmark	47	Hungary
8	Japan	48	Poland
9	Belgium		
10	Italy		
11	South Africa		
12	Germany		
13	Kuwait		
14	Qatar		
15	United Kingdom		
16	Thailand		
17	Ukraine		
18	Mexico		
19	Colombia		
20	United Arab Emirates		
21	Turkey		
22	Australia		
23	Saudi Arabia		
24	Peru		
25	Spain		
26	Philippines		
27	Portugal		
28	Greece		
29	Kenya		
30	Venezuela		
31	Guatemala		
32	Brazil		
33	Korea		
34	Finland		
35	Argentina		
36	Slovakia		
37	Taiwan		
38	Austria		
39	Romania		
40	Bulgaria		

Top Hydropower Export Markets

1	Canada
2	Chile
3	Russia
4	Venezuela
5	Colombia
6	India
7	Mexico
8	Australia
9	El Salvador
10	South Africa
11	China
12	Malaysia
13	Brazil
14	Spain
15	Philippines
16	Turkey
17	Guatemala
18	Peru
19	Portugal
20	Morocco
21	Panama
22	Argentina
23	Korea
24	Egypt
25	Japan
26	Sweden
27	Kenya
28	Thailand
29	Indonesia
30	Austria
31	Italy
32	Ghana
33	Costa Rica
34	Germany
35	Vietnam
36	Nicaragua
37	Poland
38	France
39	Romania
40	Finland
41	Bulgaria
42	Sri Lanka

Top Geothermal Export Markets

1	Kenya
2	New Zealand
3	Turkey
4	Indonesia
5	Japan
6	Philippines
7	Chile
8	Ethiopia
9	El Salvador
10	Iceland
11	Nicaragua
12	Mexico
13	Costa Rica
14	Germany
15	Guatemala
16	Russia
17	Italy
18	China
19	Australia

Top Biomass Pellet Export Markets		Top Ethanol Export Markets	
1	United Kingdom	1	Canada
2	Netherlands	2	Brazil
3	Belgium	3	Nigeria
4	Turkey	4	Peru
5	Korea	5	Mexico
6	Italy	6	Philippines
7	Denmark	7	Jamaica
8	Sweden	8	Netherlands
9	Canada	9	Finland
10	Mexico	10	Korea
11	Japan	11	United Kingdom
12	India	12	Argentina
13	China	13	Sweden
14	Russia	14	Taiwan
15	Australia	15	Australia
16	Germany	16	Ireland
17	Costa Rica	17	India
18	Malaysia	18	Japan
19	Poland	19	Israel
20	Lebanon	20	Norway
21	Greece	21	Chile
		22	Ghana
		23	Belgium
		24	Germany
		25	South Africa
		26	Costa Rica
		27	Malaysia
		28	China
		29	Egypt
		30	Colombia
		31	Pakistan
		32	Turkey
		33	Paraguay
		34	New Zealand
		35	France
		36	Thailand
		37	Ecuador
		38	Poland
		39	Spain

[1] *Bloomberg New Energy Finance, "H1 2013 Brazil Market Outlook: Has the Giant Awakened?" (July 5, 2013) pp. 3*
[2] BNEF Country Dashboard: Brazil
[3] "General Summary of New Generation Enterprises," Agencia Nacional de Energia Eletrica (ANEEL), Accessed April 2013, http://www.aneel.gov.br/area.cfm?idarea=37&perfil=2.
[4] BNEF Country Dashboard: Brazil
[5] "Programa de Incentivoas Fontes Alternativas de Energia Elétrica," Ministério de Minas e Energia, accessed April 2013, http://www.mme.gov.br/programas/proinfa/.
[6] "Country Profile: Brazil," Bloomberg New Energy Finance, Accessed 24 April 2013.
[7] *Bloomberg New Energy Finance,* "Wind – Brazil – Research Note: Brazil's 5th capacity Auction: 1.5 GW, 10 Winners, BRL 110.5/MWh PPA" (2 September 2013) pp. 1
[8] http://www.pv-tech.org/news/brazil_gains_122mw_of_solar_developments_after_state_energy_auction
[9] http://www.pv-tech.org/news/only_813mw_makes_it_to_second_a_3_auction_round_down_from_2.7gw1
[10] BNEF Country Dashboard: Brazil
[11] Presentation by Maria Gabriela de Rocha Oliveira, "Latin America Overview," Bloomberg New Energy Finance, 26 April 2013.
[12] http://www.Ex-Im.gov/newsandevents/releases/2012/ex-im-approves-32-1-million-in-financing-for-export-of-u-s-wind-blades-to-brazil.cfm
[13] Global Wind Energy Council, "Global Wind Energy Outlook 2012,"
[14] Ontario Ministry of Energy, "Ontario's Feed-In-Tariff Program: Two-Year Review Report," March 2012.
[15] Ernst & Young, "Renewable Energy Investment: Canada," April 2012
[16] There is an exception for less populated regions in Canada. (BNEF Country Dashboard: Canada)
[17] *Bloomberg New Energy Finance,* "A bout, then a drought, in the Great White North" (February 22, 2013) pp. 13
[18] Eli Lehrer, "By the Rivers of Québec: The cheap, green answer to our electricity needs," *The Weekly Standard,* Vol. 18, No. 12, 2012.
[19] USDA, Canada Biofuels Annual, June 2013.
http://gain.fas.usda.gov/Recent%20GAIN%20Publications/Biofuels%20Annual_Ottawa_Canada_6-28-2013.pdf
[20] Robin Yapp, "Chile's Uncertain Renewable Energy Future," *Renewable Energy World,* 9 April 2012.
[21] Government of Chile, *NES,* pp. 17-20.
[22] BMI; "Industry Trend Analysis – Chile Renewables: Strong Fundamentals for Growth," *Business Monitor International,* 13 February 2013 and Stephen Lacey, "Three Charts to Help You Understand Chile's Emerging Utility-Scale Solar Market," *Greentech Media,* 12 February 2013 and "Nordex Takes Part-Ownership of Chilean Wind Project," *Power Engineering International,* 11 September 2012.
[23] Government of Chile, *NES,* pp. 28-29.
[24] Yapp.
[25] Country Energy Profile: Chile – Clean Energy Information Portal (www.reegle.info/countries/chile-energy-profile/CL
[26] Bloomberg New Energy Finance, "Onwards and upwards: China's renewable targets for 2013," 23 January 2013.
[27] Ibid.
[28] Bloomberg reference in 2012 study.
[29] Global Wind Energy Council, "Global Wind Energy Outlook 2012," November 2012.
[30] Greentech Initiative.
[31] *Bloomberg New Energy Finance,* "The Future of China's Power Sector" (August 27, 2013) pp. 10
[32] Ibid.
[33] Ernst & Young, *Renewable energy country attractiveness indices,* Issue 35, November 2012, pp. 29.
[34] *Bloomberg New Energy Finance,* "Country Dashboard: India"
[35] *Bloomberg New Energy Finance,* "H1 2013 India Market Outlook" pp. 1
[36] Government of India, Ministry of New and Renewable Energy, *Annual Report: 2011-2012,* pp. 7.
[37] *Bloomberg New Energy Finance,* "India Invites Bids for 750 MW under Phase II of Solar Mission" (11 October 2013)
[38] Renewable Energy World, "Asia Report: India's Solar Market at a Crossroads," 26 February 2013.
[39] *Bloomberg New Energy Finance,* "H1 2013 India Market Outlook" pp. 6
[40] *Bloomberg New Energy Finance,* "H1 2013 India Market Outlook" pp. 1
[41] *Bloomberg New Energy Finance,* "H1 2013 India Market Outlook" pp. 10
[42] *Bloomberg New Energy Finance,* "Solar – India – Analyst Reaction: India's 3.6 GW Draft Plan for Phase II of Solar Mission" (17 January 2013) pp. 1
[43] http://www.platts.com/RSSFeedDetailedNews/RSSFeed/Oil/27891748
[44] http://www.thehindubusinessline.com/economy/article4647739.ece
[45] EurObserv'ER report (http://www.eurobserv-er.org/)
[46] Partly as a result of the European Renewable Energy Directive in 2009 (2009/28/EC)
[47] Corriere della Sera newspaper, Edilportale website
[48] *Bloomberg New Energy Finance,* "Italy Set to Cease Granting Tariffs for New Solar Projects" (June 11, 2013) pp. 1
[49] BNEF Country Dashboard: Italy
[50] BNEF Country Dashboard: Italy; and ITA's calculations
[51] Paul Gipe, "Comment: New Italian solar PV tariffs are complex and robust," *Renewable Energy Focus*
[52] BNEF Country Profile.

[53] *Bloomberg New Energy Finance*, "The end of Italy's PV FIT – but no its market" (June 18, 2013), pp. 4

[54] The European Wind Energy Association (EWEA), *Wind in Power: 2012 European Statistics*, February 2013, http://www.ewea.org/fileadmin/files/library/publications/statistics/Wind_in_power_annual_statistics_2012.pdf.

[55] Bloomberg New Energy Finance, "Feed-in-premium Policy Review," 15 January 2013.

[56] BNEF database of power plants (filter: Italy/biomass and waste to energy/announced and partially commissioned)

[57] [57] Bloomberg New Energy Finance," Italy Feed-in Premiums/Tariffs – Geothermal," Policy Detail, Updated January 15, 2013

[58] METI, "Energy Situation in Japan." December 2013.

[59] Ibid.

[60] *Bloomberg New Energy Finance*, "H1 2013 Japan Market Outlook: FIT Drives Solar Surge" (June 21, 2013) pp. 1

[61] *Bloomberg New Energy Finance*, "Solar – Japan – Research Note" (June 28, 2013) pp. 4

[62] *Bloomberg New Energy Finance*, "H1 2013 Japan Market Outlook: FIT Drives Solar Surge" (June 21, 2013) pp. 1

[63] Ibid 5

[64] *Bloomberg New Energy Finance*, "Solar – Japan – Research Note" (June 28, 2013) pp. 5

[65] *Bloomberg New Energy Finance*, "H1 2013 Japan Market Outlook: FIT Drives Solar Surge" (June 21, 2013) pp. 14

[66] *Bloomberg New Energy Finance*, "H1 2013 Japan Market Outlook: FIT Drives Solar Surge" (June 21, 2013) pp. 15

[67] *Bloomberg New Energy Finance*, "H1 2013 Japan Market Outlook: FIT Drives Solar Surge" (June 21, 2013) pp. 15

[68] Ibid, 16

[69] *Bloomberg New Energy Finance*, "H1 2013 Japan Market Outlook: FIT Drives Solar Surge" (June 21, 2013) pp. 16

[70] BNEF, "H1 2012 Japan Market Outlook."

[71] *Bloomberg New Energy Finance*, "Climatescope 2013" pp. 99

[72] *Bloomberg New Energy Finance*, "Mexico Sunshine Lures Cash for Solar After Panels Plunge" (04 October 2013)

[73] *Bloomberg New Energy Finance*, "Climatescope 2013" pp. 101

[74] "Energy Profile South Africa," http://www.reegle.info/countries/south-africa-energy-profile/ZA.

[75] Business Monitor International, "Industry Trend Analysis – Grand Renewable Plans Overly Ambitious," 7 December 2012.

[76] *Bloomberg New Energy Finance*, "S. Africa Picks 17 Clean Energy Bidders, Studies More Candidate" (29 October 20130) and "Clean Energy – Research Note: South Africa Moves Full Steam Ahead into Round 3" (8 August 2013)

[77] Ernst & Young, "Renewable energy country attractiveness indices – Issue 35," November 2012, pp. 23.

[78] *Bloomberg New Energy Finance*, "Clean Energy – Research Note: South Africa Moves Full Steam Ahead into Round 3" (8 August 2013) pp. 5

[79] Business Monitor International, "BMI Industry View – South Africa – Q2 2013," 28 March 2013.

[80] *Bloomberg New Energy Finance*, "Clean Energy – Research Note: South Africa Moves Full Steam Ahead into Round 3" (8 August 2013) pp. 4

[81] "UK Renewable Energy Roadmap Update 2012," Department of Energy and Climate Change, 27 December 2012, Accessed 17 April 2013, https://www.gov.uk/government/uploads/system/uploads/attachment_data/file/80246/11-02-13_UK_Renewable_Energy_Roadmap_Update_FINAL_DRAFT.pdf, p. 6.

[82] "UK Renewable Energy Roadmap Update 2012."

[83] "UK solar, the new kids on the ROC," *Bloomberg New Energy Finance*, 3 April 2013, Accessed 4 April 2013.

[84] This is as set out in the white paper on Electricity Market Reform and subject to parliamentary approval

[85] https://www.bnef.com/News/77224?fromGlobalSearch=135948008

[86] *Bloomberg New Energy Finance*, "Q3 2013 Wind Market Outlook" (17 September 2013) pp. 1

[87] *Bloomberg New Energy Finance*, "Global Renewable Energy Market Outlook 2013: Wind" (13 August 2013) pp. 1

[88] Goodrich, Powell, et al., *Journal of Energy and Environmental Science*, "Assessing the drivers of regional trends in solar photovoltaic manufacturing" pp. 2811.

[89] *Bloomberg New Energy Finance*, "PV Market Outlook Q3 2013" (21 August 2013) pp. 1

[90] http://www.geo-energy.org/pressReleases/2013/GEA_2013_Expanding_Global_Growth.aspx

[91] *Bloomberg New Energy Finance*, "Q2 2013 Geothermal Market Outlook" (27 June 2013) pp. 12

[92] *Bloomberg New Energy Finance*, "Q2 2013 Geothermal Market Outlook" (27 June 2013) pp. 4

[93] *Bloomberg New Energy Finance*, "Q2 2013 Geothermal Market Outlook" (27 June 2013) pp. 3

[94] *Bloomberg New Energy Finance*, "Q2 2013 Geothermal Market Outlook" (27 June 2013) pp. 2

[95] Bloomberg New Energy Finance, "Q2 2013 Geothermal Market Outlook" (27 June 2013) pp. 9

[96] *Bloomberg New Energy Finance*, "Hydropower Research Note: US Hydro in 2013 – a trickle or a flood" (9 July 2013) pp. 2

[97] *Bloomberg New Energy Finance*, "Hydropower Research Note: Sizing up global hydropower growth in 2012" (4 April 2013) pp. 1

[98] *Bloomberg New Energy Finance*, "Hydropower Research Note: Sizing up global hydropower growth in 2012" (4 April 2013) pp. 2

[99] *Bloomberg New Energy Finance*, "Hydropower Research Note: Sizing up global hydropower growth in 2012" (4 April 2013) pp. 1

[100] *Bloomberg New Energy Finance*, "Hydropower Research Note: Sizing up global hydropower growth in 2012" (4 April 2013) pp. 1

[101] Senate Testimony, May 2012. http://www.wilsoncenter.org/sites/default/files/Canadian%20Hydropower%20Senate%20CES%20Testimony.pdf

[102] http://biomassmagazine.com/plants/listplants/pellet/US/

[103] Wood chips are separate codes (coniferous and non-coniferous), and no distinction is made regarding their end use.

[104] USIPA webinar, "Europe's Growing Appetite for American Wood Pellets," held on June 27, 2013.

[105] Ibid.

[106] Eurostat.

[107] USIPA webinar, "Europe's Growing Appetite for American Wood Pellets," held on June 27, 2013.

[108] U.S. Forest Service, "The Asian Wood Pellet Markets," 2012, http://www.fs.fed.us/pnw/pubs/pnw_gtr861.pdf

[109] EU Biofuels Annual, August 2013, USDA Foreign Agricultural Service, http://gain.fas.usda.gov/Recent%20GAIN%20Publications/Biofuels%20Annual_The%20Hague_EU-27_8-13-2013.pdf (page 7)